Praise for *Tomas Young's War*

"I consider myself extremely fortunate to have known Tomas Young. I'm grateful that this powerful book of Mark Wilkerson's will allow readers to experience the strength, humor, and wisdom that this strong-willed and courageous man maintained till the very end. I miss him intensely."

—Eddie Vedder

"Tomas Young joined the army to wage war and emerged a champion of peace. The grievous injury he suffered in Iraq consigned him to a wheelchair, but from there he rose to incredible heights, raising the hue and cry against an illegal war and those who authored it. Mark Wilkerson's biography of Tomas Young is difficult but essential reading for anyone who wants to understand the ravages of war and the torment suffered by veterans and their loved ones. This book is a tribute to Tomas, written proof that profound humanity can survive the terrible crucible of war."

—Amy Goodman, host and executive producer, *Democracy Now!*

"Tomas Young's is a story that every American should know. A soldier who paid a terrible price for the crimes of his superiors, Young courageously spoke out against the illegal war that eventually took his life, and attempted to hold those who initiated it accountable. Mark Wilkerson has done a great service in rendering Young's life, and the lives of those who cared for him, in their full humanity."

–Glenn Greenwald, *The Intercept*

"Powerful, moving, inspiring. When I finished reading this book I felt it was my duty to state again that I will do whatever it takes to ensure there are no more young Americans who will have to go through what Tomas had to endure. Never again. Thank you Tomas and thank you Mark for telling his story."

—Michael Moore, Academy Award–winning filmmaker

"There is nothing more courageous than a soldier who stands up against an unjust war. Tomas Young was a true American hero."

—Tom Morello

"Tomas Young's war in Iraq lasted only five days, long enough to oblige Americans who sent him there to read this intimate, harrowing account of the life he lived after."

—**Ann Jones, author of** *They Were Soldiers: How the Wounded Return from America's Wars: The Untold Story*

"An extremely poignant statement on human vulnerability and the devastation of war."

—*Kirkus Reviews*

"Tomas Young, an army soldier paralyzed in Iraq, surmounted his injuries to become one of the most powerful and eloquent voices denouncing the war. He condemned with a righteous fury those who lied to lead us into war, including George W. Bush and Dick Cheney, and called for them to be prosecuted and tried for war crimes. He grieved for all who were injured or killed in the conflict, American and Iraqi. He spoke on their behalf. And as his health deteriorated to the point where he was unable to leave his bed he penned in his last letter one of the most scathing indictments of the Iraq war and the terrible betrayal he and his fellow veterans endured. He served as the conscience of the nation. And although his life was cut short, his is the final word on a war that should have never been fought."

—**Christopher Hedges, author and Pulitzer Prize–winning journalist** ·

"*Tomas Young's War* is a heartwarming and heartbreaking story of a courageous soldier and his family. Few books reveal the graphic details of how families deal with the catastrophic war injuries of their loved ones—Mark Wilkerson's *Tomas Young's War* does just that in a sympathetic and at times humorous way. I first met Tomas in 2005 when he and his wife arrived in hot Camp Casey, Texas, to challenge President Bush's war on Iraq, the war that had almost killed him and had left him gravely injured. Over the next eight years, as his body deteriorated, his mind remained clear about the Bush administration's lies that took the nation to war and he became an important voice for peace, not war!"

—**Colonel Ann Wright, US Army Reserve (Ret.) and former US diplomat who resigned in 2003 in opposition to the Iraq war**

"Brilliantly rendered. . . . Amid the unpleasant realities of urinary tract infections, hollow bedsores, leaking urine bags, failed erections, a collapsing marriage, and blinding loneliness, Wilkerson finds a story of love, hope, and fierce loyalty. . . . Before another commander in chief swaggers before the news cameras and declares 'Bring it on,' I want them to read this book."

—Phil Donahue, from the foreword

"As the dogs of war were howling in early 2003 and the media was simply regurgitating their hysteria, Robert Greenwald and I organized a group of celebrities, politicians, and military experts who could get attention and launched Artists United to Win Without War. We were excoriated, of course, but at least created some debate before the inevitable disaster took place. In later years, I argued that Dick Cheney, George Bush, Donald Rumsfeld, and their attending lapdogs should be required to walk naked down the main street of every American city, town, and hamlet that lost a child, or part of one, to that horrifying misadventure and suffer the ignominy they so deeply deserved at the hands of the people they had betrayed. After reading *Tomas Young's War*, Mark Wilkerson's immensely powerful, pain-streaked book, I would only amend my prescription for these war criminals by adding the requirement that they be forced to read the book, aloud, while walking those streets."

—Mike Farrell, actor, activist, and author of
Just Call Me Mike: A Journey to Actor and Activist

TOMAS YOUNG'S WAR

By Mark Wilkerson

Haymarket Books
Chicago, Illinois

© 2016 Mark Wilkerson
Published by
Haymarket Books
P.O. Box 180165
Chicago, IL 60618
773-583-7884
www.haymarketbooks.org
info@haymarketbooks.org

ISBN: 978-1-60846-650-4 (Paperback)
ISBN: 978-1-60846-591-0 (Hardcover)

Trade distribution:
In the US, Consortium Book Sales and Distribution, www.cbsd.com
In Canada, Publishers Group Canada, www.pgcbooks.ca
In the UK, Turnaround Publisher Services, www.turnaround-uk.com
All other countries, Publishers Group Worldwide, www.pgw.com

This book was published with the generous support of Lannan Foundation
and Wallace Action Fund.

Lyrics to "No More" by Eddie Vedder are used with permission; lyrics to "Until
the End" and "Stray Bullets" by Tom Morello are used with permission; lyrics to
"Soldier's Heart" by Jacob George are used with permission; quote from *Where
the Wild Things Are* is used with permission from the estate of Maurice Sendak.
Cover design by Shepard Fairey (www.obeygiant.com).
Based on a photograph by Olivier Morel.

Interior photo credits:
Danny Clinch (www.dannyclinch.com); Claudia Cuellar;
Phil Donahue; Alan Messer (www.alanmesser.com); Olivier Morel;
Eugene Richards (www.eugenerichards.com); Cathy Smith; Riley Soden

Printed in Canada by union labor.

Library of Congress Cataloging-in-Publication data is available.

1 3 5 7 9 10 8 6 4 2

Contents

For Tomas and his family

Foreword

Tomas Young's long flight from a military hospital in Land-stuhl, Germany, to Walter Reed near Washington, D.C., left his paralyzed body with the beginnings of pressure sores that exposed raw bone at spots where no oxygen reached the skin. A bald spot on the back of his head marked the place where gravity pressed it against the airplane cot on which his drugged, inert body was borne back to the States.

When Tomas finally came to, his first view was his mother's face looming over him. "Mommy," he cried, confirming a story I once heard an Army commander tell: when the soldier is hit, the immediate plea is for mother, not soon—right now. "Mommy," two syllables. Tomas was suddenly five years old. Mommy and Tomas wept together for half an hour.

The bullet that felled Tomas in Sadr City severed his spine at the T4 level. Standing next to his bed at Walter Reed, his mother Cathy Smith explained that her son was now paralyzed from the nipples down. Below the chest he is totally without control or sensation, a rag doll. Tomas can't cough, Tomas can't walk, and—in the language of the Army barracks—Tomas "can't get it up."

I am looking down at a twenty-four-year-old male in the prime of his life. He has just left a world of singles bars to enter a life imprisoned on a mattress surrounded by books, CDs, marijuana bongs,

Rolling Stone magazines, books by Hunter Thompson, and pill boxes containing scores of medications—and additional pills to correct the side effects of the other pills.

The story that follows that first meeting at Walter Reed includes a marriage that ended, a new marriage that blossomed, and a pulmonary embolism that impaired Tomas's speech and closed his hands so severely he could not hold silverware. On rare visits to the outdoors, Tomas's new wife would search restaurant space for dark corners where she could feed him without being stared at. In the last years of his life, Tomas wore a bag that captured body waste. He could no longer consume food orally; a pureed nutrient was injected into his stomach via a portal attached to his abdomen. It seemed to Tomas that all the commercials on TV were for food—delicious food.

The five years I spent creating the documentary of his life became a chapter of mine. This was a spiritual experience for all who worked on the film I created with Ellen Spiro, *Body of War*. None of us had ever been this close to an injury so severe it alters the lives of the whole family. When I first visited Tomas in his hometown of Kansas City my purpose was made clear: "Tomas, I want to show what the 'harm' in 'harm's way' really means." "I do too," he said.

What follows on these pages is Mark Wilkerson's compelling account of a warrior turned anti-warrior. The challenges met by Tomas's second wife Claudia make a love story as tender as any found on a library shelf. Amid the unpleasant realities of urinary tract infections, hollow bedsores, leaking urine bags, failed erections, a collapsing marriage, and blinding loneliness, Wilkerson finds a story of love, hope, and fierce loyalty.

Mark also brilliantly renders a true account that includes all the depression, thoughts of suicide, backaches, nausea, and vomit. Agonies never witnessed by the "bring it on" boys who boasted of their toughness by calling a war, then sending other people's kids to fight it.

Before another commander in chief swaggers before the news cameras and declares "Bring it on," I want them to read this book.

And remember, the tragedy of Tomas Young detailed in the pages that follow is the same drama now under way in thousands of homes in this country, homes occupied by a family member who, like Tomas, returned home from this unprovoked, unconstitutional, unnecessary Iraq war, troops with a catastrophic injury that changed the lives of every member of their family—forever. They are the personal tragedies unseen by the more than 95 percent of Americans who made no personal sacrifice in what was the most sanitized war of my lifetime.

Phil Donahue
New York City

Chapter I

Growing Up

In a life so deeply affected by war, it is perhaps fitting that Tomas Vincent Young didn't make it past his first day without the reverberations of human conflict leaving an indelible mark. His parents dropped the *h* from his first name, using the German spelling in a nod to the baby's German paternal grandmother, but retained the name's English pronunciation to placate his grandfather, an American. The pair met after Young's grandmother moved to the United States from Germany in the aftermath of World War II.

Tomas was born in Boise, Idaho, to Cathy and Thomas Young on November 30, 1979. It was a turbulent childhood. Cathy and Thomas divorced when their son was just two, his mother pregnant with brother Nathan. "The deal was that she would work and take care of the kids while he went to school, and then when he graduated, the situation was going to be reversed," said Tomas. "But my dad, he cheated on my mom, and so my mom said, 'I'm going to call for a moving van, it's going to be here tomorrow, and I want you to put all my shit in the moving van tomorrow.' And he goes, 'Why am I doing this, why aren't you?' To which she responded, 'Because I am leaving tonight.'" It was this fiery disposition that would make Cathy such an effective advocate for her son later in life.

So mother and son moved out, remaining in Boise for the time

being. Brother Nathan was born there, in the same hospital as Tomas, in 1982. A couple of years later, the small family moved to
Kansas City, Missouri, where Cathy's family lived. When Tomas
was ten, he and Nathan traveled to Huntington Beach, California, to live for a year with their paternal grandparents. Meanwhile,
Cathy had moved to Omaha, Nebraska, where the boys reunited
with her in 1990. "I lived a nomadic existence as a child," said Tomas—a term Cathy feels is a bit strong. "The type of men she attracted were the Bible thumpers who treated us like shit and treated
her like shit," Tomas said, "but as I've often said, she is the Bob Vila
of relationships: taking an old man who's set in his ways and trying
to change him into a brand new man. It took her a while to figure
out that wasn't the way to go."

There was a stepfather at one point who, Tomas remembered,
"ended up physically abusing me." He said he doesn't have any
memories at all of the years prior to the abuse, and that "most of
my childhood memories are not happy ones." But the bumpy ride
for Cathy and her two sons cemented a bond between them that
remained the one constant in the turmoil. This strong connection,
particularly between mother and first son, would serve Tomas well
in the future. "The bond between us, especially Tomas . . . other than
my mother, he's the person that's known me forever," said Cathy. "It
was just the three of us, kind of just getting by on a shoestring and,
what a lot of single mothers do, just milking it through, and the
boys—they were all they had, you know?"

Cathy and her children—Tomas, Nathan, and a sister, Lisa,
born five years after Nathan—finally settled in Kansas City in 1994.
"After we left Omaha, we were very poor and so we moved down
here to stay with my grandfather, bless his soul, and my aunt," Tomas said. He was fourteen.

The abuse and the lack of a strong network of friends—a result
of all the moving around—left young Tomas withdrawn. "I was a
quiet, reserved kid after this, and I didn't go out of the way to seek

attention, and I guess I still don't," he said. "I was the kid in high school that wouldn't stop by people's lockers between classes to talk—I just went from my classroom straight to the other classroom so that before the class started I had a couple of minutes to read my book. And when we would have pep rallies I would go because they were mandatory, but I would sit while everybody else was standing and cheering, reading a book."

Books left an impression on the young man, providing a map to his childhood. The *Encyclopedia Brown* series and the *Choose Your Own Adventure* series were his elementary-school staples, he recalled, before enthusiastically explaining the intricacies of the latter. Another early favorite was Maurice Sendak's classic *Where the Wild Things Are*. In middle school, it was a mix of books about sports heroes, such as Bo Jackson, and horror, à la Stephen King. In high school, he began to display a more independent streak. "Our school had a section of books that was selected by GLAAD—Gay & Lesbian Alliance Against Defamation—and so I read all those books, maybe six or seven, and I read *The Catcher in the Rye*, tried to read *Fahrenheit 451*, and read some Kurt Vonnegut—*Slaughterhouse-Five* and other stuff."

The reading, the childhood turmoil, and the close-knit family shaped a young man with a sharp intellect and a keen sense of right and wrong.

A sense of humor, too, became a distinct component of Tomas Young's makeup. Lisa was often a favorite target of the pranks her two older brothers concocted. "It was the dead of winter one time when I was thirteen, Nathan was eleven, and my sister Lisa was probably five or six," said Tomas, "and all she had on was a T-shirt and a pair of shorts, and we locked her out on the back deck and we wouldn't let her come back in until she said the word *fuck*. 'Cause she was only five years old and mom had put the fear of God into her that saying bad words was a bad thing. And she finally did it after ten minutes of being in the cold, and she came in, and Nathan and me just laughed and laughed and laughed. We were shitheads," he said, shaking his head with a smile, but then adding, "I think it had an effect, because a few years later, a kid a little older than her—he must have outweighed her by fifty pounds, fat kid—they were outside on the playground, and I guess they started fighting, and my sister pushed this kid to the ground and started bashing his head into the railroad tie that makes the boundary of the playground. So Nathan and I watched this and we see the kid run off to tell his dad, so we yell at Lisa to get inside the house, and here he comes, and his dad comes with him, and he knocks on the door and we open it, and he says, 'Hey, my son says that you two have been beating up on him.' And we said, 'No, *we* didn't do anything to your son. *She* beat him up.' And he looked at his son like, '*She* beat you up?' Shaking his head, disappointed. 'Come home.' It wasn't an easy time growing up in my family."

Tomas heard from his father every now and then. "He would send me birthday cards with money, or—they made comic-book cards that were kind of like baseball cards but they'd have like comic-book characters, and what their powers were and whatnot, so I'd get one of those every once in a while or on my birthday, and eventually those stopped." As a teen, Tomas sought out and met with his father, but there was no meaningful reconciliation. It would be more than a decade before the two would meet briefly one last time.

Tomas's interest in books during his school years led to his desire to pursue creative writing or journalism in college. The trick was how to pay for it. He wasn't particularly interested in the military, although his family had some history of military service (both of his grandfathers served in the Korean War, and his mother's stepfather was a Navy SEAL in Vietnam), but the GI Bill presented an attainable method of paying for the secondary education he desired. At seventeen he enlisted under what was known as the Split Option program, where the new recruit attends basic training during the summer between his or her junior and senior years of high school, returning for more specialized, job-specific training known as Advanced Individual Training the following summer. During the senior year of high school, the recruit serves in the Army Reserve, attending drill one weekend a month and two weeks per year. "There was no other way that I could go to college without having to pay back monstrous student loans," Tomas said. "So originally I joined for that reason. My plan was to serve my time, take my GI Bill money and go to school in Oregon or someplace. I never wanted to come back here" to Kansas City, he said.

For that first enlistment, he chose job type 71L, or Personnel Administrative Specialist—"I was told by my recruiter that that's where all the females are, and I was some horny seventeen-year-old going 'Yeah!'" he said. But not long after he graduated from Winnetonka High School in 1998, his Army career came to an abrupt end when tendonitis in his shoulder prevented him from meeting the physical requirements. Medically discharged, he found himself back in Kansas City, working at a local QuikTrip convenience store. His dreams of college seemed to be just that: dreams.

Chapter 2

September 11 and Beyond

Many of us volunteered with patriotic feelings in our heart, only to see them subverted and bastardized by the administration and sent into the wrong country.

—Tomas Young

Twenty-one-year-old Tomas Young was sleeping in on Tuesday, September 11, 2001, enjoying a day off work when, around nine o'clock, his friend Silas Mauk called him. "He told me the World Trade Center just got hit, and so I turned on the TV and sat there, watching the all-day coverage," Young recalled. His friend Roy McHugh soon came by and the stunned pair sat in silence, watching the footage of the airliners slamming into the World Trade Center and the ensuing devastation as the towers crashed to the ground. "We saw each other every day back then, before you have kids and no free time and stuff," said McHugh. "I remember going over—he was living with his mom and his grandpa, and his brother, and his other brother [Timmy, a toddler at this point] and sister—and they were all living in his grandpa's house." Young, Silas, and McHugh were close, having met as teenagers while working at Worlds of Fun, a local amusement park. "The three of us were best friends for a long

7

time, like we were all in each other's weddings and things like that,"
McHugh said. They frequently attended concerts together and made
an annual trip to Saint Louis to watch a hockey game. "Tomas and
me almost got in a fight at a Blues game, 'cause we were wearing Red
Wings stuff and the Blues fans didn't like that. . . . Tomas and I were
always kind of ornery or funny or whatever you want to call it, you
know?" McHugh remembers attending his favorite concert—Pearl
Jam at the Sandstone Amphitheater in Kansas City, October 12,
2000—with Tomas, Silas, and their friend Tiffany.

Three days after September 11, Tomas watched footage of
President George W. Bush standing atop a pile of rubble at Ground
Zero, bullhorn in hand, assuring the gathered first responders that
"the people who knocked these buildings down will hear all of us
soon!" Young, fired with patriotism and not exactly feeling constrained by the menial job he held at Kmart, called the local Army
recruiter. "When I saw the president stand on top of the World
Trade Center rubble and make his megaphone declaration, I was
moved, in a way," he said. "Yeah, I'm normally not that type of guy,
but I sat there like everybody else did on September 11 for that
whole day watching coverage. I'm sure there are a lot of people who
weren't that type of guy in December of 1941 when the Japanese
attacked Pearl Harbor, but yet they felt moved to act in that way
because of events that just unfolded."

"I kind of fostered a 'what can I do?' kind of mentality," he
recalled. "I mean, why didn't I decide to give blood, or volunteer to
do something? But I joined the Army."

The tendonitis in Young's shoulder had now healed, giving him
the opportunity to rejoin the military. McHugh recalls Tomas making a four-hour trip to Saint Louis for some paperwork to obtain
the required medical approvals, but that he was "adamant" in his
quest to enlist.

"He was always patriotic," McHugh recalled, adding that Tomas had enlisted with a friend the first time he'd signed up back in

high school. "I remember we were driving back from Overland Park from a movie, and they were trying to yell out the window at some marines, and the marine guys were hanging out of their car, flashing their marine shirts, and they're flashing their Army T-shirts, and stuff like that." But there was a more practical element to Tomas's decision, too: "I think he joined the Army because obviously he was upset about what happened to the country," said McHugh, "but he was also looking for something to do with his life, talking about just regular, crummy, nowhere-going jobs he was working."

Nearly a month after the September 11 attacks, as Tomas was putting the administrative wheels in motion to facilitate his enlistment, a bombing campaign marked the beginning of war in Afghanistan, the sanctuary of 9/11 mastermind Osama bin Laden, his al-Qaeda network, and the hardline political ruling party, the Taliban. The ramp-up to war meant that the US Army's demand for combat arms jobs—chiefly infantry, armor, and artillery—skyrocketed. While recruits like Tomas, who attained a score of 110 on the general/technical portion of the ASVAB (Armed Services Vocational Aptitude Battery) recruitment test, could normally pick practically any job they desired, the Army's need to funnel recruits into combat arms constrained Tomas's choices. He remembers his choice of jobs came down to "tanker and infantryman." Young saw himself as "the GI Joe–type character," so he chose infantry.

By early February 2002, Private Young had arrived at Fort Benning, Georgia, for initial processing—shots, haircut, paperwork, and equipment. Nine weeks of basic training began on Valentine's Day, followed by five or six weeks of additional infantry training, whereupon Young received his blue infantry cord and other accoutrements to signify his status as an active infantry soldier. He subsequently shipped out to his permanent duty station of Fort Hood, Texas, expecting to be deployed to Afghanistan in short order.

Just a week or two before Young resumed his Army career, his commander in chief indicated that he had his eye on other targets, too. Afghanistan appeared to be simply the first. "Our war against terror is only beginning," remarked President George W. Bush in an ominous State of the Union speech on January 29, 2002. Bush identified an "Axis of Evil," citing North Korea, Iran, and Iraq as "regimes that sponsor terror" and posed "a grave and growing danger." He only briefly addressed the first two nations before focusing on Iraq:

> Iraq continues to flaunt its hostility toward America and to support terror. The Iraqi regime has plotted to develop anthrax and nerve gas and nuclear weapons for over a decade. This is a regime that has already used poison gas to murder thousands of its own citizens, leaving the bodies of mothers huddled over their dead children. This is a regime that agreed to international inspections then kicked out the inspectors. This is a regime that has something to hide from the civilized world.

The US focus on Iraq—and its likelihood as a potential target for military action—intensified as the months passed.

Tomas Young arrived at Fort Hood in early June 2002. He was assigned to Alpha Company, 2nd Battalion, 5th Cavalry Regiment (2-5 Cav), a mechanized infantry unit whose typical mode of deployment was the M2 Bradley Infantry Fighting Vehicle. Tomas had expected to hit the ground running upon his arrival, with some type of immersive combat training geared toward counterinsurgency fighting in the Middle East. He was surprised, therefore, when upon his arrival he observed that "we trained for war rarely. We spent most of our time marching or cleaning in the motor pool. So it was a frustrating thing for me." This wasn't what he'd signed up for.

When his unit did train, Tomas noted that it was inappropriate, World War II–based conventional combat training, which would prove ill-suited to the war soon to be waged in the Middle East: while training geared toward conducting combat operations in an urban environment was useful, the conventional "overwhelming firepower" approach proved ineffective in a counterinsurgency setting, where winning over the populace was key to turning the tide. The troops of 2-5 Cav received no training on the people of the Middle East or their beliefs and customs.

Tomas, observant and unafraid to voice his concerns, quickly earned the disdain of his superiors by questioning the infrequent and inappropriate training. Considered impertinent, he was assigned extra duties such as picking up trash and sweeping sidewalks. "I was just tasked with a large amount of busy work," he recalled, "because they couldn't formally punish me for simply asking questions."

When new recruit Riley Soden arrived at Fort Hood about three months after Tomas, he was warned by his superiors to stay away from the disrespectful private. "They roomed me right next door to him in the barracks," Soden recalled, "and they told me that he was one of the guys I shouldn't hang out with," citing Tomas's impertinence and excessive drinking. "It turns out he's one of the best guys I ever knew and we became real good friends, so . . . they didn't really know what they were talking about."

The pair quickly hit it off. "The very first day that I was in the barracks, Tomas knocked on my door and said, 'I hear you're from Kansas City,' and he had a beer, and we just sat down and started talking," said Soden. In addition, the two men were the same age—twenty-two, about four years older than many new Army recruits—and shared many of the same interests. "We liked the same music, and I think we were kind of interested in doing the same things, and we just became pretty good friends and started hanging out together, you know, formed a bond." The pair listened to their favorite music together—"a lot of alternative stuff at the time, a little heavier, like Tool, Rage Against the Machine, Pearl Jam," Soden recalled. They were also fans of professional wrestling. The Sports Dome, across the street from the barracks, often hosted wrestling and other entertainment events, which Soden and Young frequently attended.

On October 11, 2002, just a couple of months after Tomas and Soden's first encounter, the US Senate approved a resolution authorizing the use of military force against Iraq. The resolution marked the culmination of a shift in the government's approach to war—from retaliation to preemption—which had been gathering momentum as the year progressed. The approach had first been articulated in Bush's "Axis of Evil" speech back in January and was reinforced in his commencement speech at West Point in the summer. The "Bush Doctrine" was officially outlined in a National Security Strategy document which was issued in September. The strategy referred to a new policy of acting "against emerging threats before they are fully formed," and "taking anticipatory actions to defend ourselves, even if uncertainty remains as to the time and place of the enemy's attack." The Senate voted seventy-seven to twenty-three in favor of going to war, clearing the path for a preemptive invasion of Iraq. Just a few months later, Secretary of State Colin Powell delivered his now-famous "weapons of mass destruction" speech to the UN Security Council, during which he expressed absolute certainty that Iraq was housing weapons of mass destruction and that they posed a threat sufficient to justify preemptive attack. Despite protests across the globe by millions of antiwar demonstrators, the war in Iraq began on March 20, 2003.

As the likelihood grew that he would be deployed to Iraq, Tomas became increasingly concerned with this new and unexpected development. "Right after 9/11, I saw the president talking about how we were going to smoke the evildoers out of their cave and bring them to justice," he told *Billboard* magazine in 2008. "I guess I've watched too many *Law & Order* episodes. I thought you followed the evidence, went and took out the guilty. When we were attacked by the Japanese at Pearl Harbor, we didn't go after the Chinese because they looked sort of similar."

Tomas and Riley Soden spent many evenings discussing the new focus on Iraq. "We talked about it a bunch and how we kind of expected to go to Afghanistan at first," said Soden, "and then when all the stuff started coming out on Iraq we realized that we were going to be going there, and there was kind of a double-edged sword, 'cause you want to go where you think the people who attacked you came from, but you signed this contract with the military and they kind of own you at that point. So I wanted to do the right thing and support my fellow soldiers but neither one of us were real pleased about where we were going. Tomas was very vocal about it. I just kind of realized that I didn't have much of a choice."

In addition to speaking out about the new development, Young's response was to withdraw and self-medicate. "I was one of the only people that he talked to or even hung out with at that point," Soden recalled. "He started drinking real heavily to kind of try to cover it up and help him deal with where he was going and all that."

Tomas's dismay over his impending deployment to Iraq spiraled further. He sought professional help from the battalion doctor. "I tried to get antidepressants to balance my feelings or something," he recalled, "and the doctor said he couldn't give me any antidepressants or medications like that until I'd seen the chaplain. And I thought, well, I'm not a very religious person, but if that's what I need to do to get my drugs to get my mind right, then I'll do that. And I went to the chaplain, and I told him all my problems about how I joined to go to Afghanistan and I felt that Afghanistan was the right fight, and I was very upset and despondent about going to Iraq. And he looks at me and puts his hand on mine and says, 'Son, you'll feel better when you get over to Iraq and start killing Iraqis.' And I'm thinking, 'Well, okay—you officially put me in the 'atheist' column!'"

Having received this stunning response from the chaplain, Tomas returned to the battalion doctor, who prescribed Prozac. It didn't work.

Tomas's heavy drinking continued. He went back to Kansas City the following New Year's Eve, visiting a Westport bar with his brother Nathan, Riley Soden, Roy McHugh, and other friends to ring in 2004. "We went down to Westport—we used to do that every year, and we'd always rent a hotel room down there so we wouldn't have to drive back," McHugh recalled. "I was dating this girl, and then we kind of stopped seeing each other and I asked her if she wanted to go out for New Year's, and I never heard back from her, so I was like, fine. So I asked out a different girl for New Year's, and they both showed up! It was the only time I was ever cool, you know? So I had a group of friends at one bar with one of the girls, and a different group of friends at another bar with the other girl! And every time I would leave the bar that Tomas was at, he would drink my drink. So he was smashed, and smashed early, like before ten o'clock—out of it." Tomas soon disappeared, leading to a frantic search by Roy (who'd been found out by his two dates at this point) and Tomas's younger brother. "We found his sweater, and like parts of clothes and stuff strung out all over Westport," McHugh recalled, "and we finally made it back into the room, and I think he was curled up with a bottle of Jack or something in the bed, but he was always just funny that way. He was always a good time."

It was at another bar during this same period of leave that Tomas would meet his future wife. "We were at a bar with my buddies Silas and Roy and their girlfriends, now their wives," Tomas said, "and Silas goes, 'I've never had an Irish Car Bomb—I want to go somewhere where I can get an Irish Car Bomb.' And Roy and I said, 'Hey, there's an Irish bar down the street.' So we went down there, and I saw this girl, and I was like, 'Where the fuck do I know her from?,' but I didn't go over and talk to her or anything. So we did our Irish Car Bombs and ordered another beer and she came over to me at my table and said, 'I don't know if you remember me, but I'm Brie Townsend,' and I went, 'Ahh! Brie Townsend! I was trying to figure out who you were over there.'" Young remembered Brie from high school. "I had kind of a little crush on her, 'cause she was kind of the hippie alternative skater chick that I was attracted to at that time," he said. Townsend gave Young her number and told him to give her a call sometime. "And I said, 'Well, I'm getting ready to deploy to Iraq sometime soon, so I don't know either when I'll see you, or if I'll see you again.'"

Back at Fort Hood, Tomas continued to explore options to remedy his despondence. Perhaps using his incomplete 71L Personnel Administrative Specialist training as a selling point, Tomas approached his chain of command about switching jobs from a line infantry squad to a more clerical role with Headquarters Company. Just a month or two before his unit shipped out to the Middle East, Tomas was swapped with an NCO (noncommissioned officer) in the S1 (Personnel) shop. He assumed some clerical duties in addition to taking responsibility for the company's M113 communications vehicle and equipment. "Because the guy who had that job at Fort Hood had a combat patch, they figured they'd rather trade an experienced guy for me, 'cause I wasn't a model soldier by anyone's imagination," Tomas said. "I did my job but I always questioned, and I was a smartass and they hated that."

"He shifted from Second Platoon to Headquarters," Riley Soden said. "He was in charge of the radios and working in the office and all that. That was his way of trying to stay out of combat. Which obviously didn't help in the long run. But it was a good idea."

In hindsight, Tomas didn't agree. "Going to Canada wasn't as in vogue among dissenting soldiers at that time, so I transferred into a job in the company clerk's position from the infantry line platoon," he later recalled. "I thought I was going to put myself in the safest position possible. It was a horrible plan."

Meanwhile, on February 8, 2004, eleven months after the onset of what was known as Operation Iraqi Freedom, President George

W. Bush appeared on NBC's *Meet the Press* and had the following exchange with Tim Russert:

> Russert: The night you took the country to war, March 17 [2003], you said this: "Intelligence gathered by this and other governments leaves no doubt that the Iraq regime continues to possess and conceal some of the most lethal weapons ever devised."

> President Bush: "Right."

> Russert: "That apparently is not the case."

> President Bush: "Correct."

Chapter 3

Black Sunday

It's almost unfathomable, the price that is paid because of this theory about going to war and letting democracy blossom from the rubble of Baghdad, which is the story that was sold to the American public and then pushed through without a proper debate. And then to see the reality of it, it changes you—and that's what you want everybody to remember.

—Eddie Vedder

A couple of weeks before his unit's deployment to the Middle East, Tomas received news that his grandfather had died. He was granted a week of bereavement leave and went back to Kansas City to be with his family. Toward the end of the week, after the funeral and family gatherings were over, Tomas is careful to point out that he asked his mother, "Mom, I know that I'm only up here because Grandpa died. If you need me around to comfort you or anything, I understand. But would you be OK if I called this girl Brie?" Then he called the girl he'd met a few months earlier, the last time he was home. They had time for a single, memorable date before Tomas had to leave for Fort Hood. "Three days later," said Tomas, "I was preparing my gear to ship out."

On the day he departed for Fort Hood, Tomas's high-school friend Roy McHugh left town, too, but on a far more desirable mission: a weeklong cruise with friends. When he returned the following week, he had two voice messages from Tomas. The first was from Texas. "He called and left me a drunk voicemail saying that he was having a good time back in Texas, and he had forgotten that I was gone on a cruise," McHugh recalled. "The other one was a couple of days later, and it was just a way different sound to his voice." Young was calling from Kuwait. "On that voicemail, he sounded like—I don't know, he sounded different from what was him," McHugh said. "I don't know if he was scared or tired, or anxious, or what, but it was just like a big difference in his voice." McHugh remembered Tomas calling him a few more times during his stay in Kuwait. "We talked about a lot of nonsense—'Remember this time, remember that time' kind of stuff, trying to take his mind off of it . . . I'm sure it wasn't the easiest place to be."

2-5 Cav shipped out to the Middle East via charter flight in mid-March 2004. "We got to Kuwait at like three in the morning," Tomas recalled, "and went straight into this briefing room about how it was bad to be alone, always be with a buddy, and don't smoke outside 'cause it could serve as a signal." After the briefing, the soldiers were driven by bus to their temporary base. It was still dark when they arrived. "The next morning you realize that Kuwait is in the middle of a huge desert and so there's nothing for miles in any direction of our base," said Riley Soden. "It was a surreal feeling."

The new arrivals staged in Kuwait for a couple of weeks, getting acclimated to the scorching temperatures, preparing their equipment, and waiting for their vehicles to arrive by sea before the looming deployment to Baghdad. "They feed you there, and they give you all the equipment that you need to go into the city with, basically," Soden recalled. "We unpacked stuff and got everything ready. At this point, Tomas and I ran into each other now and again, but we didn't see each other much 'cause we were doing different things, you know. He was in Headquarters and I was in Alpha."

Part of preparing for deployment into combat meant a steady stream of briefings about the team's mission. Unfortunately, that mission kept changing. "When we were back at Fort Hood they told us one thing, we get to Kuwait they told us something else, and when we got to the base in Baghdad they told us a whole other thing," said Soden. "Initially it had been we were going to go take out terrorists, and then once we got to Kuwait it was like, well, you're going to be a quick reaction force if anything happens in the city, and then when we get to Baghdad, they said well you're going to be kind of the police force and just run patrols, so that's what we prepared for. It was a little nerve-wracking."

"And trust me," Soden added, "we either argued or disagreed with most of the things that were happening, 'cause we kept saying, 'Well, I don't think that's going to work,' and they'd say, 'Too bad— deal with it,' but that's the Army, you know, that's how it works."

Another early briefing focused on the emerging threat of improvised explosive devices, or IEDs. "They showed us a bunch of pictures of what the IEDs could look like," recalled Soden, "and it was—it turned out to be *everything*. Like, anything you could think of was an IED. It really just kind of made you more nervous, really—they could have just left that out."

Despite that general feeling of uneasiness, life in Kuwait for the soldiers of 2-5 Cav was as comfortable as could be expected. The troops stayed in air-conditioned tents, with showers and bathrooms available in nearby trailers. They had limited email, Internet and phone access, and even a Subway and a Burger King. Tomas remembers the base having "a little PX [post exchange] that sold magazines, water, soda, and this Middle Eastern iced tea, and near-beer, and cigarettes and tobacco and CDs and little portable DVD players, and all that stuff." One thing he couldn't purchase was alcohol. In accordance with the country's laws, there were no spirits available; the only beer for sale was alcohol-free. "I was like, why would you drink near-beer for the taste—why?"

Tomas thought often about Brie and found himself constantly writing letters to her. "I wrote her all this time, but I couldn't send anything to her because I didn't have a return address," he said. "And so I had all these letters stuffed in my pockets and everywhere. There was one twenty-seven-page letter that I had actually written her that just detailed all my life up to then."

The final few days in Kuwait were spent preparing the newly arrived vehicles for the deployment into Iraq. Tomas remembers that his platoon, the last to leave, was tasked with "cleaning up everybody's trash they'd left behind."

Private First Class Tomas Young's arrival in the Middle East in March 2004 marked exactly one year since the beginning of Operation Iraqi Freedom, a period during which the US military rotated nearly the entire force in Iraq—approximately 130,000 troops—at once. This period of turnover and instability presented the Iraqi resistance, which had been relatively quiet in the preceding months, with a prime opportunity to wreak havoc. Sure enough, the insurgency intensified in scope and violence in the wake of the changeover as an increasingly agitated populace took advantage of the inexperienced replacement units and shook itself loose of the grip of the US military.

On March 24, the Army's 82nd Airborne Division turned over responsibility for the city of Fallujah, just west of Baghdad on the Euphrates River, to the Marine Corps. A week later, on the day Tomas flew from Kuwait to Baghdad, four American security contractors working for Blackwater in Fallujah were killed and mutilated. Two of the contractors' bodies were burned and hanged from a bridge while frenzied crowds cheered and chanted. Footage and photos of the gruesome scene were widely broadcast, reminding American viewers of similar horrific images from a decade earlier, when dead American soldiers had been dragged through the streets of Mogadishu, Somalia.

In Baghdad, the popular Shiite cleric Moqtada al-Sadr was beginning to prove particularly troublesome. On March 28, the Baghdad-based Shiite weekly newspaper *Al-Hawza* was labeled a mouthpiece of the increasingly bellicose al-Sadr by American Coalition Provisional Authority (CPA) chief Paul Bremer, who ordered the paper closed for sixty days. This development caused outrage among al-Sadr's followers, who demonstrated outside the doors of the paper's Baghdad office, which had been chained shut by the US military. Another demonstration took place in Sadr City, a huge Shiite slum on the northeastern corner of Baghdad named after al-Sadr's father, a cleric who had been murdered at the order of Saddam Hussein five years earlier.

Meanwhile, 2-5 Cav was moving out to Baghdad to begin an expected twelve- to fifteen-month deployment. Tomas's vehicle, an M113 Armored Personnel Carrier outfitted with communications equipment, was trucked to the Iraqi capital along with the battalion's Bradley Fighting Vehicles while Tomas made the 400-mile trip on a C-130 aircraft. After a brief stop en route for fuel, Tomas arrived at Baghdad International Airport on March 31, 2004. He then was transported to his assigned location, Camp War Eagle, a twenty-mile journey through the heart of Baghdad and Sadr City in the back of a 2.5-ton truck known as a Light Medium Tactical Vehicle (LMTV). The latter left a lasting impression. "It was like, this is not a good place where I'd want to hang my hat," Tomas recalled. "The buildings looked very dilapidated. The entire time I was there I don't think I saw one house that was basically like a Middle Eastern version of this house—just a regular house, or a luxury house. It was all tenements." Young also vividly recalled the smell of burning garbage. Garbage collection in the sprawling urban slum had ceased recently; it didn't take long for the waste of the city's 2 million occupants to accumulate and create major sanitation concerns.

New to this stage of the war in Iraq (and, for most of them, to combat in general), the soldiers of 2-5 Cav had no idea that they were about to be dropped into a buzzing hornet's nest. In fact, they expected precisely the opposite. "We had heard when we got there that there hadn't really been any violent conflict in the area that we were going to, Sadr City, in a while," Riley Soden recalled. "When we actually landed and got to the base, the guys we were talking to said they hadn't done anything in six months. So that kind of calmed you down a little bit." The only recent excitement had occurred when a lone Iraqi civilian fired a few shots into the air one day. It turned out that he was drunkenly celebrating his birthday.

Camp War Eagle, nestled alongside the northeast corner of Sadr City ("It was kind of a shock—you're *right next* to the city," said Soden), wasn't yet a year old. The camp was still under construction when Young's battalion arrived. "It seemed like it was a little in disarray," said Soden. "The guys that were there had just gotten there, and they had only been there a very short time, 'cause they were still building the barracks." The habitable portion of the barracks was occupied by the unit that was preparing to rotate out. Still officially in control of the area, they maintained control of the chow hall and were afforded priority on the use of the phones and the Internet. Meanwhile, 2-5 Cav slept in tents and ate C rations prepared in a mobile kitchen. As the driver of the company's M113 communications track vehicle, Tomas was afforded a little more privacy than many of his fellow soldiers, as he slept in his assigned vehicle. Apparently, this was pretty much all it was good for. "It was constantly in the shop—it never worked," he recalled.

Isolated on the island of his commo job in HQ platoon, Young often found himself assigned menial tasks such as guarding equipment while the battalion prepared to assume command the following Sunday, April 4. "[I was] guarding stuff. Watching it.

Mostly I listened to CDs from back home and talked with other guys," he said.

He also gained a quick distaste for some of the members of the outgoing unit. "I would see guys come back from patrol laughing about how they opened a bag of Skittles and scattered them in the Iraqi dirt and laughed as the Iraqi kids ran over and ate the dirty candy, or they'd chew and they'd spit their dip into a soda bottle, close it up and throw it onto the street and laugh as the Iraqi kids drank the chewing tobacco. That was where I'd first flown in and my thought was this is what happens when you send a generation raised on *Jackass* and *Grand Theft Auto* off to war. 'Cause they were just fucking kids."

On April 1, 2-5 Cav's first full day in Iraq, Riley Soden manned the gun atop the lead vehicle on his company's first patrol into Sadr City. It was the first time he'd ridden as a gunner in a Humvee; he'd received no training or even briefings about how to fire from a vehicle. The patrol consisted of regular Humvees without any protective armor. "Our first patrol was pretty intense, because we didn't really know what to expect," Soden recalled. "It's so busy and packed— and then within the first hundred feet of the gate, I saw everything they showed me on that video that could have been an IED. And so I was just nerve-wracked, you know, and then once you kind of realize, oh well, if it's going to happen it's going to happen, and there's not much you can do about it, then you just kind of relax a little bit."

That first patrol was uneventful, but tensions in the area continued to escalate. Al-Sadr, in his weekly Friday sermon on April 2, spoke of attacks by "the occupiers" and instructed his followers to "be on the utmost readiness and strike them where you meet them." The next day, CPA chief Bremer again dealt a blow to the influential firebrand and his followers when top al-Sadr deputy Mustafa Yaqoubi was arrested in Najaf, inciting further uprisings among the previously quiet Shiite population. *Newsweek*'s Melinda Liu described tensions reaching a fever pitch that same day, with the ominous sight of "10,000 men marching on the streets of Sadr City, including black-clad al-Mehdi militiamen wielding ritual scimitars," while "colleagues armed with rifles assumed sniper positions on the rooftops." Battered Sadr City was a powder keg, primed and ready to blow.

On the following day, April 4, Tomas Young found himself assigned to bag duty—guarding duffel bags—as 2-5 Cav prepared for an assumption-of-command ceremony scheduled for that evening. Soden had resumed his role as gunner in a small convoy that escorted an officer through downtown Baghdad to a government building in the Green Zone.

Early that morning, Moqtada al-Sadr issued a statement: "There is no use for demonstrations, as your enemy loves to terrify and suppress opinions, and despises people. I ask you not to resort to demonstrations because they have become a losing card and we should seek other ways. Terrorize your enemy," he implored, "as we cannot remain silent over its violations."

His followers, invigorated from the previous day's massive demonstration in Sadr City, duly obliged. Within hours of this call to arms, thousands of al-Sadr devotees launched coordinated attacks against the US-led occupying forces in several locations south of Baghdad, and in Sadr City itself. By that evening, fighters from al-Sadr's ten-thousand-strong militia had seized control of all seven Iraqi police stations in Sadr City. They set up roadblocks using garbage, junked appliances, cars—anything they could use to obstruct traffic and hinder any intervention from the US military. Many of these obstacles were set alight, filling the streets with smoke.

A small patrol consisting of four Humvees and nineteen men from Charlie Company, 2-5 Cav, was in the city at the onset of the chaos and quickly became a convenient target for the hostile throng. The soldiers took casualties, lost two vehicles, and became pinned down in an alley. The ensuing military response to this situation was what saw Young and Soden deployed into the cauldron.

Soden had just returned to Camp War Eagle from his mission to the Green Zone early that evening when the news came in. "We had just got off our vehicles, put all of our gear away, and we were eating chow that night and that's when the call went out that someone had taken fire in the city, someone from Charlie Company," he recalled. "And all the radios started blowing up, you know: Alpha, Bravo, Charlie . . . and we headed out."

Tomas Young's memories of that violent day are jumbled and hazy. "I don't remember a lot about that day," he cautioned before offering his recollections. He remembers that he was still guarding duffel bags when the call went out. "I was listening to my CD player and my squad leader said, 'You've got to get your gear on and go do this mission.'" Tomas recalled protesting, "But Sergeant, I'm watching these bags," to which his squad leader responded, "I'll watch the bags for you, you've got to go on this mission."

"And so I went out," Tomas recalled. "I got sent out on an all-hands type of mission, which is funny 'cause the guy who sent me out on that mission was an E7 and had a combat patch, but said he couldn't go outside the wire because he had back problems and shoulder problems." Although he was part of a mechanized infantry unit, Tomas found himself climbing into the open bed of a 2.5-ton truck—an LMTV—without even a canvas covering to at least make it difficult for a sniper to take aim at the truck's contents. Tomas was one of at least twelve in the back of the truck (his recollection was of about twenty soldiers, while other accounts and a photograph place the number at a dozen). Regardless, it was cramped,

---

* Why didn't 2-5 Cav use their armored Bradley Fighting Vehicles that day? "The Bradleys are technically not supposed to be used in an urban environment," said Riley Soden. "If the enemy force is large enough and well armed, they will send them to provide cover fire for ground troops. On the day we were injured they only had reports of small-arms fire, deeming the Bradleys unnecessary. They were deployed after the initial battle that we were in. Since we were an occupational force, they resisted ever letting the Bradleys out of the FOB [forward operating base]. It's hard to win the hearts and minds with such an aggressive symbol rolling through the streets."

difficult to move, and practically impossible for each soldier to take a meaningful defensive posture. "I was sitting with my legs crossed Indian-style. Well, not sitting—I was laying on my back on the floor to make room for more people," he recalled.

Soden quickly found himself out in the city again, back in his familiar spot as Humvee gunner. "We were actually going in to set up a medevac spot, a rally point," he said. "Having been in the city earlier, it was real busy, but then we turned a corner to be on that main road, there was *nobody*. And that's when I knew it was bad. When all the civilians are gone, you realize that something bad's about to happen."

Meanwhile, the cramped LMTV containing Tomas Young lumbered out into Sadr City. Only a block or so along the north-south road known as Route Delta, they began taking fire from the windows and rooftops of the buildings which lined both sides of the street. "When I tried to shoot out of the side of the truck, I couldn't maneuver my weapon very well and so therefore didn't fire a shot," Tomas recalled, citing the cramped quarters, and "because all I saw were women and children who were running from the firefight. But I did see guys with AK-47s go down, so I knew that my guys were doing what they were supposed to." But Tomas's fellow soldiers in the back of the open truck were sustaining injuries at an alarming rate. Staff Sergeant Robert Miltenberger, the ranking NCO present and Young's former squad leader, scrambled to coordinate return fire and administer first aid.

Meanwhile, Soden's convoy had driven into an ambush. "They started shooting and we returned fire, and we actually forced our way through that area, through an actual kill zone, even though we had a bunch of flats, and took a casualty in that process, and took another one when we turned the corner. And then, as we were trying to evac the area, we took some more casualties and that's when I got shot. It went through the side of my vehicle and hit me in the ankle." The bullet blew a hole in the back of Soden's left foot, fracturing his heel and damaging his Achilles tendon.

At around 7 p.m., Tomas, still sitting cross-legged and jammed into the back of the LMTV, suddenly went numb as he was hit by an AK-47 round from above and to his left. The bullet had entered below Young's left collarbone, tearing through his lung and spinal cord before exiting just below his right shoulder blade. He had been in Iraq for five days and had never discharged his weapon.

"When I got shot, it didn't really feel like I had gotten shot, 'cause I didn't feel anything," he recalled. "I just dropped my weapon and I was very dazed, so I just thought a concussion grenade had gone off, or some kind of grenade that's meant to incapacitate you for a few minutes. But I tried to pick up my weapon and couldn't. At all. And I knew something bad was going on, and so I tried to yell, 'Somebody, just finish the job, take me out,' but my lungs had collapsed, so all that came out was a very hoarse whisper." Miltenberger, who had already been attending to multiple casualties with severe gunshot injuries, scrambled over to render first aid while the dwindling handful of unharmed soldiers in the back of the truck returned fire. "I remember him telling me I wasn't going to be paralyzed when I said, 'I'm going to be paralyzed,'" Young recalled. "He said, 'No, you're not, don't worry about it.' He tried to keep me in good spirits." The bullets continued to rain down. Tomas was hit again, this time shattering his left knee. He felt nothing. Then he passed out.

The LMTV had slowed to a crawl. It was separated from the rest of its convoy and taking heavy fire. While there is no doubt that the truck had sustained damage from enemy fire, Young insisted that it was prone to overheating anyway. "The truck I was in wasn't supposed to be out on missions," he recalled. "It was on water and food detail, to bring water and food to the soldiers inside the wire, and it overheated several times—and in fact that day it was scheduled to be in maintenance because of the radiator. And so we're driving, and the first thing I hear is the radiator died again—and later it was written the radiator had been shot out, and that wasn't the case. Because if the radiator had been shot out, the vehicle couldn't have moved at all while we're in this very unfriendly war zone, and more bad things would have happened."

The supply truck, full of injured soldiers and littered with bullet casings, discarded first-aid dressing packets, and blood, slowly exited the firefight and finally broke down on the way back to Camp War Eagle. "We made it to a different part of Sadr City, which fortunately for us was friendly to American troops, and since the truck couldn't move any more, one of the few people in the truck that wasn't injured got out and commandeered an Iraqi tour bus," Tomas said. "Next time I woke up, I was being carried over to an Iraqi tour bus by two Iraqi citizens. I can't remember much after that."

Tomas was still unconscious when they made it back to Camp War Eagle, where the injured were being triaged. Soden was also in the triage area. "It was pretty crazy, they had us all laid out by litter, kind of by severity of injury," he recalled. Eight US soldiers died that day and more than fifty were injured in the fighting, in what the *New York Times* called "one of the worst single losses for the American forces in any firefight since Baghdad was captured." It is estimated that several hundred Iraqis died. All but three of the soldiers in the back of Tomas's LMTV were injured, many of them seriously. The next time he woke up, he was in Kuwait. He had no recollection of how he got there.

Tomas could recall a few flashes of memory after that. "I remember waking up in the Army hospital in Kuwait and this attractive young female medic came to me with a specimen cup and it had a little barbell in it, and I looked at her and said, 'Oh, you had to take that out.' I had my penis pierced at the suggestion of an ex-girlfriend. And she said, 'I would have liked to have met you before we deployed,' and I was a little doped up, so I said, '*Yeeeaaah*, I would have liked to have met you, too!' And I passed out."

While in Kuwait, Tomas was prepped for surgery to remove shrapnel and bone fragments from his back and for a process called decompression surgery, or laminectomy, where the lamina—the back part of the vertebra that covers the spinal canal—is removed, allowing the soft tissue in the spinal canal to expand, or decompress, reducing the risk of further damage. "I remember going down a hall on a gurney to the O.R. and I remember looking up at the ceiling and seeing strips of flypaper that were just covered with flies," he said, "and I remember thinking, "*This* is super-sanitary—I wouldn't be surprised if I get some kind of infection."

He was then placed in a medically induced coma.

Soden, meanwhile, had no idea that Young had even been out in Sadr City, let alone seriously injured. "We were only told about our convoy. I didn't even realize the other convoy, the one that Tomas was on, was leaving," he said. "We thought we were the only ones going to the city." Soden had been taken to the large military hospital in Baghdad to receive initial treatment for the gunshot wound to his ankle. (He subsequently endured months of additional treatment and therapy.)* "One of the NCOs came in with a list, and he'd just start reading off the names of the people that were wounded or whatever, and he said 'Young,' and I said, 'Is that Tomas?,' because there were two Youngs in our company, him and a kid named Preston Young. And at the time the guy said, 'No, I think it's Preston. He'll be fine.' Preston had gotten mildly—he got grazed." It wasn't until a couple of weeks later that Soden realized that it was actually his friend Tomas who had been catastrophically injured.

---

* Soden was later flown to Germany and then to Fort Hood for surgery. It took three months before he could walk unaided, after which he spent another three months in physical therapy.

Chapter 4

April 2013, Kansas City

Some days I have good days and some days I have bad days like everyone else. It's just that my bad days are worse than most people's.

—Tomas Young

A typical day for Tomas in April 2013 begins with his wife, Claudia Cuellar, giving him a tube feeding and administering his medications. She empties the colostomy bag and the bag that the urine goes into from his Foley catheter. Over the course of each day he takes a dizzying array of pills, alongside the powerful narcotic Dilaudid, administered in liquid form through his pain pump:

Warfarin (Coumadin)—a blood thinner
Omeprazole—for acid reflux and stomach acid
Potassium—if Tomas's potassium gets too low, his heart could stop
Cranberry—to battle urinary tract infections
Baclofen—for muscle spasms
Tizanidine—muscle relaxant
Midodrine—for low blood pressure
Venlafaxine (Effexor)—antidepressant

Levetiracetam—twice a day to prevent seizures
Vitamin D—helps the body absorb calcium
Xanax—for anxiety and insomnia
Loratadine (Claritin)—for allergies
Simethicone—chewable, for gas and bloating
Lorazepam (Ativan)—for nausea
Ondansetron (Zofran)—for nausea
Quetiapine (Seroquel)—for sleep
Zolpidem (Ambien)—for sleep

Tomas lives in a three-bedroom ranch house in northern Kansas City, Missouri. It's a relatively compact place with beige vinyl siding, white trim, and barn-red shutters. There's a blue minivan out front with a "dog lover" magnet on the back. At the top of the concrete wheelchair ramp that leads up to the front porch is a table, upon which sits a copy of the Dalton Trumbo book *Johnny Got His Gun*—a story, nearly eighty years old, about a man who suffers horrific injuries as a result of war. Next to the front door there's a framed picture of a wild-eyed, red-bearded Tomas peering out from under a Thor helmet. Tibetan prayer flags, strung across the porch railing, and an Earth flag on a pole mounted to the house flutter in the breeze.

It's early afternoon, my first time meeting Tomas. Claudia answers my knock at the door almost immediately and greets me with a broad smile. Petite, with long, straight dark hair pulled back to reveal a gold bindi on her forehead, she ushers me into their living room, where three of Tomas's antiwar veteran friends are sitting and chatting. The entryway and living room are cluttered with books, pictures, posters. There are so many framed posters that there isn't enough room on the walls. Several stand on the floor, leaning against the wall, stacked sometimes three or four deep. On the wall are posters by artists Shepard Fairey and Alex Grey, including Fairey's poster for the *Body of War* film featuring Tomas and his brother Nathan. There's an *Easy Rider* movie poster signed by Dennis Hopper, Peter Fonda, and Jack Nicholson. A Johnny Cash portrait, signed "To Tomas—Johnny Cash." Several signed Pearl Jam concert posters. A Tool concert poster. A black-and-white poster of a young Rage Against the Machine. A Bill Hicks movie poster, under which is a small picture of George Carlin.

The mantel houses more personal keepsakes: a photo of Tomas and Claudia on their wedding day. An embroidered "Dysfunctional Veteran" baseball hat that belonged to Tomas's grandfather. There's a shelf on the other side of the mantel with the Virgin Mary and the Buddha, and a photo of a man in Buddhist robes (Claudia explains that this is Chögyam Trungpa, a Buddhist teacher). Against the shelf lean a ukulele from Hawai'i and a Martin acoustic guitar.

The home is filled with books. A few hundred are in the living room, stacked by the fireplace and under the window that looks out onto the porch. There's Maurice Sendak's children's classic *Where the Wild Things Are. Mortality* by Christopher Hitchens. *Shambhala: The Sacred Path of the Warrior* by Chögyam Trungpa. A wealth of art and literature.

Tomas's room is in the back of the house, with a Batman sign pinned to the closed door. Inside, Tomas is taking a nap. Claudia explains that he tends to wear down as the day goes on, so we may not have much time together today. While Tomas is resting, Claudia shows me his Hunter S. Thompson room: a guest bedroom turned into a shrine to the original gonzo journalist, replete with copies of Thompson's books; framed posters, including the iconic "Thompson for Sheriff" peyote-fist 1970 campaign poster; a skull; and photos of the author. Tomas later tells me—only partly joking, I think—that the room is a good litmus test for his guests. If they don't like the Hunter Thompson room, there's a good chance he's not going to like them.

A muffled call from Tomas summons Claudia to the bedroom. While she is tending to him, I venture back to the living room and talk to the visiting three Iraq war vets. They've known Tomas for several years; one is also a photographer. We talk about our experiences in the military and how we came to know of Tomas's story. I show them the copies of my two books that I've brought for Tomas, and we talk a little about music.

Claudia soon emerges and tells us that Tomas is ready to see us now. As we file down the hallway toward his room, I notice his desert-camouflage Army field jacket, with its 1st Cavalry Division shoulder patch, hanging from the back of an open closet door.

The four of us, plus Claudia, file in. Tomas is there, reclined in his hospital-type bed, wearing his loose-fitting Batman T-shirt. He is bearded, his face drawn. His blue eyes are vivid but heavily lidded, as if he's exhausted. A blanket covers his legs, which are barely more than bone and skin, withered and atrophied from nine years of paralysis. Now thirty-three years old, Tomas has been paralyzed from the chest down for nearly a third of his life.

Tomas greets us. I don't know if I can shake his hand; fortunately, he offers his. I grasp and shake his right hand with both of my hands, as he can't grip. His fingers are cool and straight. "Nice to meet you, finally," he says, smiling and nodding politely. I later learn that his left hand is a little more adept at grasping, so we do a modified handshake from now on. His voice is nasal; it appears to be hard for him to enunciate every word. His breathing is congested and labored.

On the bed next to Tomas is a tray containing a cup holder, an ashtray, cigarettes, a lighter, a cell phone, and a PlayStation controller. A gray push-button switch lies close by, its wire snaking over the side of the bed to the pain pump. A bench and couch to either side of the bed provide room for guests. A flat-screen TV is mounted to the wall at the foot of the bed. Elsewhere on the wall are images of comic-book and sports heroes: Batman, Walter Payton, the Boston Red Sox. There's a lift frame attached to the ceiling above his bed to aid Claudia in transferring him from bed to wheelchair. A dark sheet hangs over the window behind Tomas's bed. It's quiet. The colors back here are subdued—the sheets on the bed are gray, the walls in the bedroom dark blue, nearly black. It's the opposite of a hospital room—no bright lights, no beeping sounds. The only similarities are the bed, the pain pump, and the constant interruptions.

The excruciating abdominal pain that Tomas began to experience a year ago is still there, kept at bay—at times—by the drugs. "Usually the pain comes from here," he says, pointing to his lower left abdomen, right where his stomach is. "I've been to many doctors and finally one admitted that sometimes pain just is there and there's no reason for it. I mean, I've had a good portion . . . I've had my gall bladder removed, my appendix removed, and my colon removed, so there's not really a whole lot in there anymore. So—we don't know where the pain is coming from. It's just there." He describes the pain as "like somebody has got steel-toed boots on and they're kicking me in the stomach. It hurts quite a bit."

Since he moved to hospice care, Tomas's pain is managed by a pain pump, which currently feeds him about 8 milliliters of Dilaudid every hour. He says the Dilaudid completely eliminates the pain at times, but occasional waves still break through. "I have what is called a basal rate, which is the 8 milliliters per hour that I get. Then I have what's called the bolus, where I just press this gray game-show-like button to get like a milliliter of medicine for breakthrough pain. Every once in a while, the pain gets stronger or the body gets used to that much medication and so the pain overtakes the medication and they keep having to come out and up it, and . . . I don't know, if it gets too severe they may change the pain medication entirely to a different kind or whatever, but this one that I'm on now is I guess the top one."

The pain pump makes it tough for Tomas to get out of bed. "It was okay before the pain pump," he says. "I mean, 8 milliliters an hour may not sound like a lot, but it's a very concentrated dose. It's not like they're adding saline to it or anything else, it's just the straight Dilaudid. And so it does tend to make me very tired, and subsequently I have a fucked-up sleep cycle. I'll fall asleep maybe at seven-thirty, eight in the evening, nine at the latest, and wake up at like four or five in the morning and just be ready to go." He also naps frequently throughout the day. In addition to the grogginess, there's also the fact that whenever he ventures out, he has to lug the pain pump along with him.

When the pain is under control and he's not sleeping, Tomas passes the time by listening to music, playing video games, or watching baseball, old TV episodes, or movies using Amazon Instant Video or Hulu through his PlayStation 3. "I'm pretty much well set up here," he says, nodding to the TV and the speakers. Back before the pain pump and the colostomy, he got out more frequently. "I would go out to eat—I don't do it, obviously, anymore 'cause there's no need—and occasionally I would go to the movies, but . . . I had two choices. If the auditorium was big enough, then I could take the elevator to the top, where they have a couple of handicap seats. . . . I could either sit up at the top, right next to the very loud speaker, or I could sit up at the very front, and," he says, straining his neck upwards as if looking at a movie screen above him, "neck pain. With the big-screen setup I have and no lights, I can have marijuana and cigarettes and watch a movie, so . . . it's a much better situation."

Tomas's breathing is often quite labored. He explains, "I find it very hard to quit smoking cigarettes, and when I was able-bodied and I smoked I was able to run and get that out of my system, and even when I was in the manual wheelchair, but now that I'm sedentary all the time, even when I'm in the chair all I do is move a joystick, so I'm constantly congested with mucus." Tomas has been unable to cough since the spinal cord injury, because his abdominal muscles are paralyzed. Claudia has to help him cough up any mucus, basically by giving him a shove in the abdomen with her open hand.

John, a caregiver, comes by at three every Monday, Wednesday, Friday, and Saturday to aid with Tomas's care—emptying colostomy or catheter bags, feeding, etc. In addition, Steve, the hospice worker, comes out every Monday, Wednesday, and Friday to change the cartridge of Dilaudid in Tomas's pain pump. "It has a key and is set with a certain dosage as prescribed by the doctor," Claudia says. Steve also changes the dressings on the pressure sores on Tomas's hips and changes the needle on the pain pump at regular intervals.

Later, while Tomas is resting, Claudia escorts me to the kitchen. There's a bulletin board on the wall displaying childhood photos of Tomas with his brother, his mother, his dog. Tomas's many medications stand on the counter next to the sink, along with a mortar and pestle. Claudia soaks the pills in tap water to soften them before she grinds them up and dispenses them in water through the feeding tube. One wonders if such a combination of drugs doesn't introduce one or two new ailments, given the cocktail coursing through his system.

"He mechanistically functions," reflects Claudia. "I feed him liquid food through a tube, like vanilla and sugar, basically; that's the nourishment that's trying to fill in his pressure sores. He needs nourishment to rebuild his body somehow. And then he does empty waste, but he doesn't feel better, you know? It feels Frankenstein-ish. When I look at him, when I step back and I just look at all the stuff they've done to him, and he doesn't feel better. Then what's the point? You know. It looks like mutilation to me."

In addition to the assortment of pharmaceuticals, Tomas uses marijuana to alleviate nausea and muscle spasms. Some spinal cord injury (SCI) patients say it's the best anti-spasticity drug out there. "Before I enlisted in the Army I smoked marijuana recreationally, 'cause I enjoyed it," Tomas tells me, "and after I was injured I found things out on the Internet and through other sources that marijuana has been used medicinally since the ancient Chinese days and before Christ." He tells me that there are even some anecdotal stories of Jesus using it. "And so after realizing that it had health benefits, I then went on to discover that the vaporizer they use now is a healthier form of it, because instead of lighting a joint or a pipe, like you would a cigarette, and therefore emitting carcinogens into your lungs, the vaporizer just kind of bakes the herb and lets the vapor come through. It's what the cancer patients use, and the AIDS patients, and the other people who have it prescribed in the open-minded states. It gives them a healthier option."

Because the use of marijuana, medicinal or otherwise, is illegal in Missouri, Claudia has to purchase the drug from a local street dealer.

Back in the bedroom, Claudia puts a cigarette between Tomas's lips and lights it. He takes only a few long draws on it before clumsily stubbing it out on the ashtray with his uncooperative fingers. She gives him a water bottle after taking the lid off and taking a sip, so he won't spill the contents.

His friends from the military make some small talk with him as they prepare to say goodbye. They're laughing and joking with him, but I sense an air of awkwardness, of unease. This very well could be the last time they see their friend. They discuss the upcoming opening of the George W. Bush Library in Dallas. Tomas comments that there will probably be a sizeable supply of coloring books there, and that if anyone asks, they'll say they're for when George stops by—and that he never could color between the lines.

After the three friends say their goodbyes, Claudia shows them out, leaving me alone in the room with Tomas. I pull out the two books I brought for him. He looks on with interest and says he has trouble holding books and flipping pages since his brain injury. I also brought him—of all things—a Hunter S. Thompson poster, destined for addition to the stacks on the floor.

We talk about how he's feeling, what's been happening recently. "I'm feeling pretty good, thanks to the pain pump," he says. He mentions that Eddie Vedder visited him last week, spending the night in Kansas City on the way home to Seattle from a short Pearl Jam tour in South America. Tom Morello was here recently too. Others who've stopped by include former US Army colonel and State Department official Ann Wright, who resigned in protest of the Iraq war, and actor Mike Farrell, of *M*A*S*H* fame—both outspoken activists who oppose the war in Iraq.

Tomas talks about the "reunion" scheduled for next Monday, to be filmed for ABC's *Nightline*. He'll get to see Staff Sergeant Miltenberger for the first time since Black Sunday. The March 5, 2007, episode of *Nightline* had shown that Miltenberger continued to face his own demons. He'd been awarded the Silver Star for somehow managing to return fire while providing life-saving first aid to the wounded in the back of the truck, but he haltingly told Martha Raddatz that the award meant "nothing," adding, "I was just doing my job. I don't know why they picked me out of anybody else on that truck." Miltenberger, fighting back tears, said he felt guilty for "lying to the soldiers—you know, you're supposed to keep them calm and stuff, tell them . . . 'Don't worry about it, you're not hurt that bad.'" He recalled Tomas "saying, 'I'm paralyzed, I'm paralyzed.' I said, 'No you're not—everybody's just laying on you.' There was nobody laying on him."

Miltenberger has been haunted by what he saw that day. He slept in his blood-soaked uniform that evening, refusing to change clothes. A few months later, he had walked out into the still-hostile streets of Sadr City, opened his body armor, and shouted for someone to kill him. "I tried to call him up and I couldn't ever get hold of him, to say, no, I don't hold anything against you, you were just trying to keep me from getting overly upset," Tomas says. "So—you are forgiven. But apparently I get to say that now, because next Monday there's going to be a small reunion here with Staff Sergeant Miltenberger and two other guys from the company that I don't recall getting along with very much, or talking to a whole lot, or anything like that. So it seems to me like they want fame and attention."

Despite the fame and attention, after enduring more than nine years of steadily worsening disabilities and pain since the day he was shot in Sadr City, he's had enough. Tomas has decided to end his life. After his first wedding anniversary next week, he plans to stop taking nutrition from his feeding tube and, he says, "one day . . . go away."

Chapter 5

Waking Up at Walter Reed

A hospital alone shows what war is.

—Erich Maria Remarque, *All Quiet on the Western Front*

Cathy Smith was at work around midday on Monday, April 5, 2004, when she received a phone call from a member of 2-5 Cavalry's rear detachment back at Fort Hood. Tomas had sustained a gunshot wound, Cathy was told—but, maddeningly, there were no further details. An agonizing eight days of misinformation and confusion ensued before she could gain any clarity on the situation.

"That evening, someone called me from Washington, D.C., to tell me that my son had been severely injured, and because of that, the Army would take care of all my travel arrangements," Cathy began. "They needed my social security number, blah blah blah—I thought it was a scam. So I said, give me your phone number—I'll call you back. I called them back and they told me that he was in Kuwait still—he had been transferred to Kuwait—that's all the information they had, and that as soon as they had more, they would talk to me about my travel information, you know, where I needed to go. I probably would have to go to Germany. The next day, the rear D called and told me that they believed that he had a knee injury—a gunshot wound to the knee—and a neck injury. And that's all they knew that next day. During the next five days I was told . . . he went from being severely injured, to not severely injured, back to severely injured. During the whole time, I talked to I don't know how many different people trying to get information as to where he was—they still kept saying he was in Kuwait, they were stabilizing him."

"Finally, on Saturday," she continued, "I was told that he was no longer considered severely injured, so they weren't going to take care of my travel arrangements. I still didn't know where he was, still didn't know what was going on, still thought he was in Kuwait, but I knew if he wasn't severely injured he would have contacted me. He would have called me. So I started making phone calls—and I had probably a hundred names by now I'd gone through that I'd called, you know, trying to find out what was going on—finally got hold of a Captain Cummings at Landstuhl in Germany, and he said that Tomas had already been in Germany for a week—and I could have been there with him. *For a week.* And that they had already sent him to Walter Reed. And that was on Sunday I found that out."

It had been seven days since Tomas had been shot. Cathy still had no information as to the extent of her son's injuries. "I still had no idea," she said. "I spent probably three days in my bathrobe, not taking a shower, not eating, just sitting by the window, waiting for the government car to pull up and tell me my son was dead." On Monday, Cathy finally received official notification that her son was indeed at Walter Reed Army Medical Center in Washington, D.C. She flew out there immediately.

That Monday evening, upon arriving in Washington, Cathy remembers walking across the lobby to the medical intensive care unit at Walter Reed and seeing her son for the first time. "That's when they had just removed him from his medical coma," she recalled, "and I still didn't know the extent of his injuries. I just remember walking across and seeing him, all just a million tubes and everything, just . . . instruments and . . . here's my twenty-four-year-old baby, says 'Mommy' and starts crying."

When Tomas awoke from his medically induced coma, he had pneumonia and weighed only seventy-five pounds. His shattered left knee was grotesquely swollen from the gunshot wound and the subsequent surgery to remove bullet and bone fragments. His upper torso bore the fresh scars of the bullet's entry and exit wounds, the surgery to clean the debris from the bullet's trajectory, and the pressure-relieving laminectomy. A feeding tube transported nutrition directly into his stomach, a tracheostomy aided breathing, and an IV provided the necessary medications, including a heavy dose of morphine for pain.

Tomas doesn't remember Landstuhl at all. He was comatose from Kuwait all the way through to Walter Reed. The first thing he remembers seeing after coming to was his mother, who had just arrived. "I just started bawling like a baby," he recalled. "I don't care how tough you are—I don't care if you hated your mom and that's why you went away to war, but if you come home shot and paralyzed, as weak and as vulnerable as you've ever felt in your whole life, and you see your mother, you just . . . fall to pieces."

It was April 12, 2004.

It wasn't until the following day that Cathy and Tomas were finally informed as to his physical condition. "No one would tell us what the extent of his injuries were," Cathy recalled, "and finally the next day a nurse—not even a doctor, but a nurse—finally told me that he had a complete injury to the spinal cord and they had done a laminectomy, and that, you know, it was permanent, and this was the way it was, there was no swelling that was going to go down."

"Complete" meant that the cord had been completely severed. Individuals who suffer complete spinal cord injuries experience no sensation—pain, temperature, position sense, touch—and no motor function below the level of the injury, which, in Tomas's case, was the T4 thoracic vertebra, in his upper mid-back. He was paralyzed from the chest down.

Tomas said he wasn't surprised at the news that he'd never walk again. "I knew in the truck that I was paralyzed," he said, "so when they said I was paralyzed, I was kind of like, 'Ahhhh, I knew this.' So I was ready for that. It didn't really have any major effect on me."

Maybe the morphine helped soften the blow of this devastating news, or maybe Tomas was simply in denial at the time—a normal part of the grieving process—but it still felt like an unreasonable response. "I think I moved past that part relatively quickly in my mind," Tomas offered when I asked for further details on his mindset, "because one of the lessons I've learned from the rocky road of my life is that I can't dwell on the negatives for too long or else I'll become extremely depressed. And so I just moved on through it and accepted it as . . . why bother, it wasn't my choice, so . . ." When I pressed further, explaining that he made it sound so simple, Young admitted, "Well, it wasn't really."

No, it wasn't. Undoubtedly, the morphine clouded Young's memory, as his mother remembered him being predictably devastated and inconsolable upon receiving the news that he was now paraplegic. Cathy remembers him wanting to kill himself "every day, all day long" for the first two weeks. "Every day, all day long," she recalled. "That's all he talked about. He cried and cried and cried—he hated me because I wouldn't kill him, and hated the nurse because they were doing this, and hated the doctor."

Cathy's response to Tomas's pleading was blunt, but exactly what he needed to hear. "It just sounds really cruel," she said nine years later, "but it was kind of the same thing that we went through just recently, you know—you can't use your arms and legs, and you want to. . . . I'm not going to kill you, and you can't do it, so you best buck up. You know—get over it."

Whether it was the grieving process running its course, the various medications Tomas was given, Cathy's tough-love responses to his pleading, or the combination of all of these, Tomas slowly began to emerge from his despair and to wrap his mind around a new series of challenges. "It took time," Tomas said, "but eventually I realized that my situation wasn't going to change or get better, so I should get used to how my life was."

Getting used to how life was for Tomas would be his new focus, a daily struggle with pain as well as physical and psychological challenges. In addition to Tomas being immobile and without any physical sensation from the chest down, his bowel, bladder, and sexual functions were all affected, along with many other functions that he'd taken for granted. "You know, you see a guy who's paralyzed and in a wheelchair, you think, 'Oh, he's just in a wheelchair,'" Tomas explained. "You don't think about the stuff inside that's paralyzed. I can't cough, because my stomach muscles are paralyzed, so I can't work up the full coughing energy. I'm more susceptible to urinary tract infections, and there's a great big erection sidebar to this whole story."

Despite the morphine, there was still pain to deal with. When he woke up from the coma, Tomas felt sharp, needlelike pains in his legs, which felt like they were still crossed as they had been at the moment he was injured in the back of the truck. "My legs felt like they were still Indian-crossed, in that style, although I could look at them and see that they were straight," he said. "And so I asked a doctor, I said, 'Why is this happening? Why do I feel this way?' And he goes, 'Well, when you get shot and paralyzed, your body takes a picture of how it was situated, of what you were doing before you were paralyzed.' And so for like the next two or three weeks, my legs felt like they were crossed. And," he said, furrowing his brow and prolonging the words for emphasis, "*it hurt*."

During his initial recovery period, Tomas said he also suffered from pain "in the back where [the bullet] exited, 'cause that was where it was ripping the bone and skin and everything. For about a month and a half after I got shot, that would hurt."

Meanwhile, Tomas's younger brother, Army Private Nathan Young, had just joined his new unit at Fort Campbell, Kentucky. In the midst of a ceremony marking the unit's return from Iraq, Young received a call from his mother, who told him she'd just found out that Tomas had been injured. Thus began the harrowing weeklong rollercoaster, as the misinformation flowed. Once it was determined that Tomas was at Walter Reed, Nathan's chain of command gave him a four-day pass to visit his brother.

When Nathan told Cathy he'd been granted only four days, she assumed what she refers to as "mama bear" mode. "She talked to somebody at Walter Reed," Nathan recalled, not exactly sure what was said, but still marveling at the results. "And a general called my unit and said, 'Nope, you're getting ten days TDY [temporary duty].' My commander called me in and said, 'I don't know who the hell you talked to or how you did it, but you're getting ten days TDY.'"

Nathan arrived at Walter Reed a couple of days after his mother. "He was in ICU," he said, "and they had just woke him up from his medically induced coma, and . . . yeah, he looked pretty rough, he just had a bunch of tubes going in and out of him, and he didn't really know where he was, he was all doped up off the morphine, and . . . it was pretty bad." He recalled that Tomas was too sedated to even recognize him. "Yeah, there was no reaction. I mean, he was . . . so gone off morphine that there was no reaction whatsoever."

Cathy was a rock for Tomas during this period. She stayed at Fisher House, a nearby residential facility for visiting family members. "She would come to my room before visiting hours started, and stay till after visiting hours were over," Tomas recalled. A former EMT, she applied equal amounts of medical training and fiery stubbornness in advocating for her son, tirelessly holding vigil at his bedside. "Well, I would stay until one, two o'clock in the morning, stay until they would kick me out, leave for a couple of hours, do laundry or whatever at the hotel, and then come back quickly, because I saw so many wrong things—they just had to wait for the doctor for *everything*."

In talking with others, she also discovered she wasn't the only victim of misinformation during the notification process. "I met a bunch of amazing people at Walter Reed. . . . I met amazing parents. There was one kid in there, they told the father that his son was dead and he had a heart attack. And then, two days later, they called and said his son *wasn't* dead, but that he had a traumatic brain injury."

"She really fought for the VA to expedite my claims so I'd get paid," Tomas added, "and got the Army to promote me to E4 [Specialist], which I should have been, so I could get E4 retired pay." Cathy also came up with an idea to try to lift her son's spirits.

"My mom said, 'Well, you've always been into politics, and now you're in Washington, D.C., who do you want to meet?'" Tomas recalled. "And I was under heavy sedation right then. . . . [Ralph] Nader possibly got George Bush elected in 2000, but he was the only presidential candidate at the time that wanted to bring the troops home from Iraq, so I said I wanted to meet him."

Cathy duly contacted Nader's office. Nader promptly agreed to visit, and asked longtime friend and television talk-show host Phil Donahue if he would accompany him. The pair had known each other for years. "I just worshiped Ralph," said Donahue, who recalled that in the twenty-nine years of the *Phil Donahue Show*, Nader was the most frequent guest. "He would always draw a crowd," he said. In April 2004, Donahue was visiting Nader's office in Washington, D.C. "He said, 'A mother at Walter Reed wants to meet me—do you want to go?' I said, 'Yeah,' I had never been to Walter Reed. Immediately I said, 'Yeah.' So I think I flew back like a week or two later, and off we go to see this young man lying in bed in a room at Walter Reed."

Tomas recalled a flurry of activity around his hospital room before and during the Nader visit. "A bunch of doctors showed up to talk to Ralph Nader," he told *Smith Magazine* in 2008. "I had trouble getting care before that, but that day I could have had cancer because there was an oncologist present, I could have been a pregnant woman because I think there was someone from obstetrics there, just to talk to Ralph Nader."

Tomas didn't remember much about the actual visit due to being heavily sedated at the time, but he did recall that Nader "brought me all these books that he'd written and talked to my mom a whole lot, and he brought his friend Phil Donahue, who talked to me more."

"He was as white as the sheets," Donahue recalled, still visibly shaken by the memory nearly ten years later. "He was whacked out on morphine, you could see his cheekbones, and as I stood next to the bed, his mother explained his injuries to me—that Tomas is a T4, he's paralyzed from the nipples down, and twenty-four years old, he's impotent, prime-of-life male—and I thought, people should see this. This is the most sanitized war of my life. The president said, 'You can't take pictures of the coffins,' and the whole press corps said"—he shrugs indifferently—"'OK.' Less than 5 percent of us made a personal sacrifice for the Iraq war. We did not see the pain."

Donahue was deeply moved by the visit. "I was speechless," he said, "and that's not a usual thing for a talk-show host."

In May 2004, after spending about three weeks in the ICU at Walter Reed, Tomas was transferred to the Jefferson Barracks division of the VA Medical Center in Saint Louis, a unit specializing in spinal cord injuries. It was at Jefferson Barracks that his girlfriend Brie visited him for the first time. "Sometimes she would lay in the same bed as me," Tomas recalled. He was finally able to deliver the letters he'd written to her back in Kuwait and Baghdad. It was in Saint Louis that Brie told Tomas she wanted to marry him. "I didn't ask him," she said matter-of-factly in *Body of War*. "I just thought he should know."

Tomas's old friend Roy McHugh and his dad—"My dad always liked Tomas," McHugh said—also visited him in Saint Louis. "I was anxious to see him and it was kind of hard," he said. "He was in horrible shape—you could kind of see it in the movie, too, but he had this bald spot on his head just from where his head had been resting 'cause he had been sedated so long. He would just randomly fall asleep during midsentence, and I'd hang out and he would wake up like twenty minutes later and he'd be talking about the same thing he was talking about twenty minutes ago, like he didn't even know he fell asleep. I'd never known anyone that this had happened to, that had been paralyzed—I didn't even know anyone that had been shot, you know? I didn't know what to expect. But when you talked to him, he was just like, if he was sitting down and I was sitting down it was just like it ever was, you know? It was pretty messed up, but he was still himself. And he had a lot of problems and he'd get sad, and he'd get depressed. He'd get mad."

McHugh visited Young in Saint Louis on several occasions, plus the pair would often reminisce on the phone to help ease Tomas's mind. But, inevitably, the conversation would return to his current situation. "He was real brave about it," McHugh recalled. "Like, I remember he kept making references to *Kill Bill*—remember when the chick woke up from the coma and she was just trying to move her toe? It was like he was trying to do that, and I remember he wished that he could just use crutches, then he wouldn't feel so weird about being in the wheelchair, he'd feel more normal if he could do that. I mean, we didn't really openly talk too much about being sad and what was going on there, but he knew what it was, and he was taking a lot of medication after what happened to him, stuff for depression."

Other pressing issues threatened to further complicate Tomas's health if not addressed immediately. Two critical issues were linked to the functioning of his bladder and bowel. Young no longer had any control over either function and had to learn how to manage them, a messy, embarrassing, and emotionally distressing ordeal. Adding to this already complicated process was the constipation caused by painkiller intake and a general lack of bodily movement, plus nausea and diarrhea, all common among SCI patients.

"He was always really open about talking about what was going on," said McHugh. "I remember when he got shot, I was thinking about things for him that I never even thought about for myself. I mean, I was like twenty-three, twenty-four, and I never thought about, you know, having kids and stuff like that, and I'm like, man, I don't even know if he can. He had, I remember, a whole bunch of people there at the hospital trying to help him, like he had to learn how to do this catheter thing. The only thing I knew about a catheter, I thought you just put that tube in and it just stayed there, but he had some kind that you put on and off, and it kept falling off on him a lot of times, and it would just be a mess. . . . He couldn't control his bowels, he would have gas or something and it would be loud, and I think he'd be, you know, embarrassed, so that he'd just apologize up front and explain that he couldn't control it, especially when he was around people he hadn't met."

Initially, Tomas used an external catheter—essentially a condom with a tube at the tip, which ran to the collection bag that was strapped to his leg. Since they are not inserted into the urethra, external catheters present less discomfort and a lower risk of urinary tract infection, but they have their own issues, chiefly skin irritation and failure to stay in place, resulting in leakage.

Bowel programs typically consist of a combination of suppositories, manual removal of stool from the rectum (digitally, by the patient, wearing a lubricated latex glove), and digital stimulation of the sphincter. It's a daily process that often lasts an hour or more. Medications such as stool softeners, bulk formers, laxatives, and enemas are also employed, depending on the patient's specific needs. Thus, two critical body processes to which Tomas previously had given little regard became huge obstacles to comfortable daily living.

Tomas didn't remember attending, or even being offered, any counseling, coping classes, or any other kind of psychological help to help him deal with grief and adjust to his new life. He did, however, remember physical rehab at Walter Reed and in Saint Louis. "I remember my initial forays into physical therapy were for me to be moved from my bed to this specialized chair which I just sat in for two or three hours and then was transferred back to my bed," Tomas said of his experience at Walter Reed. "So I didn't really do any physical therapy while I was at Walter Reed. Then when I was transferred to the Jefferson Barracks in Saint Louis, that was where I did rehab, like learning how to get dressed and learning how to brush my teeth and to eat again, and just some leg stretching, trying unsuccessfully to learn how to do wheelies to get up curbs and things." He recalled the rehab at Jefferson Barracks as "the only one that I actually got into . . . the one that showed me the most improvement."

Transitioning from the feeding tube, which had been inserted during his coma, back to solid food involved an unpleasant experience with pureed food. "What they would do was they would puree up corn, and then reshape it to make it look like corn on the cob," Young recalled. "Or they'd take a piece of meat and grind it up and then reshape it to make it look like a piece of meat. I couldn't eat that stuff, and the deal was, if I didn't get two thousand calories by eating during the day, then they were going to have to give me this feeding tube. So I said, 'That's fine with me, I'll take the feeding tube over this baby food shit.'"

McHugh remembered other unique difficulties. "I remember all sorts of weird things he had to learn," he said, "like he couldn't wear pants with back pockets in them forever 'cause I suppose it would've given him sores or something, from sitting on them."

Another thing that struck McHugh during his visit was that Tomas "was like the only young person there. Like, the guy he was sharing the room with was from the Vietnam War era. There was no one to—I don't know, you can talk to older people, but it's kind of hard to relate to people that are a lot older than you. And I remember being freaked out because the guy that he shared a room with, he'd been paralyzed for however long, and he was back in the hospital 'cause the guy had a water bed and when he was laying in it he couldn't feel it, and it burned him so bad, they put him the hospital."

One can only imagine a young Tomas looking on, thinking, *Is this what I get to look forward to?*

But VA hospitals around the country were once again beginning to fill with young men and women. The events that culminated in Tomas's injury marked the beginning of a new phase of violence in Iraq. Casualties soon began to pour in. While about 2,700 US service members were wounded in the first twelve months of the fighting, more than 8,500 would be wounded in the ensuing twelve months—triple the number injured during the first year. Tomas was at the front end of a huge wave of more than 26,000 service members who would be treated for wounds sustained in Operation Iraqi Freedom during the four years spanning from 2004 to 2007. Another 3,422 US service members suffered fatal injuries in Iraq during that same period, nearly seven times more than the 553 who had lost their lives during the first twelve months.*

Cathy agreed that the Saint Louis facility had "a lot more older guys. They would put him in these therapy groups and always felt that group therapy would help. But it was a bunch of older guys. Trying to find a paralyzed Iraq veteran that Tomas could relate to didn't exist, you know. That's how I ended up getting into Military Families Speak Out. And through that, that's how we came to find Tomas's group, Iraq Veterans Against the War."

"There were two guys on my floor who were my age," Tomas recalled. "One had been in a Marine unit, and they had taken over one of Saddam's palaces. They were swimming in his pool and he dove in this pool and was made quadriplegic after hitting his head on the bottom. He had to have this special bed that sent vibrating sand all through his bed so that he wouldn't get bedsores ... because

---

* The website www.icasualties.org keeps a running count.

he couldn't roll himself over. And there was another guy who was in advanced training for the Navy and he skipped out on one of the classes and got on his motorcycle and drove into the back of a truck. . . . I was the only actually injured-in-war vet. The closest thing I had was the guy who had hit his head, but I don't consider that a war injury. That could happen here at home. Most of the others were car accidents."

The people Tomas remembered relating to most while at Jefferson Barracks were a couple of orderlies who worked on his floor. "We used to talk a whole lot," he said. One of the orderlies "would give me weed, and so I would go downstairs, buy a can of pop, poke some holes in it with a safety pin, and put a big hole in it, then go outside to the picnic area and smoke some weed, throw the can away, and put the weed in your little fanny pack, then go back upstairs and—goodnight."

On July 16, 2004, Tomas Young was discharged from inpatient care for his spinal injury. He and his mother were taken aback when they received the news that he was to be sent home just 103 days after he had been wounded.

They set off for home in Cathy's car, his new wheelchair folded in the trunk. "I remember them giving us my bag of medications and my wheelchair, and my shower chair, and we went off," Tomas said. "And I remember . . . just out of the parking lot, near Target, I shit my pants. My mom had to take care of it. My mom was a big hero those first few years."

Chapter 6

Back Home

And the walls became the world all around.

—Maurice Sendak, *Where the Wild Things Are*

One of the first things Tomas Young did when he returned to Kansas City was to call Sergeant First Class Powell, the NCO who had ordered him to grab his stuff and climb aboard the LMTV on Black Sunday. "I didn't get hold of him, I had to leave him a message," Tomas recalled. He left an abrupt, "Hey, Sergeant Powell—it's Private Young. I'd just like you to know that if I could, I'd like to shit down your throat. Bye."

A particularly striking scene in *Born on the Fourth of July,* Oliver Stone's cinematic rendition of Ron Kovic's memoir, is when Kovic returns home in his wheelchair and is greeted by friends and family for the first time. It's a searing, awkward moment; unmentioned truths flash over people's faces as they are confronted with the jarring reality of seeing their loved one in an unfamiliar position of weakness and vulnerability.

Tomas remembered this scene from his own life—the varied reactions of close friends and family upon seeing him at home for the first time, paralyzed. "The adult ones, or at least the ones that were decent poker players, they acted like it didn't bother them," he said, "which was the way I wanted people to react. And then some . . . mostly women in the family, would bawl over me and tell me it was God's plan. And I got sick and tired of hearing that."

He didn't just hear it from family members. Not long after he'd returned home, Tomas remembers "these Baptist kids walking down the street in front of my house, and they were talking to my brother and sister and her friends. And they were trying to tell them about the wonderful life that you'd have if you accept Jesus into your heart, and I rolled out there and I said, 'So, people have been telling me that this is part of God's plan. If you guys seem to have such a direct line to the old man, tell him what plan am I supposed to ascertain from this? What am I supposed to do now? What's the next part of the plan?'"

For the first few months back home, Tomas lived with his mother in Liberty, a few miles northeast of Kansas City. Because Cathy was living in a split-level home, her son could only access a small portion of the floor space using his wheelchair. "My mom had built him a little area there in the living room and put up a divider," Nathan recalled. "She tried to make it as comfortable as she could for him."

"I stayed in a hospital bed right behind the couch so I could look at the TV," Tomas said, adding that he watched a lot of baseball games that summer. "I got special permission to smoke cigarettes and marijuana in the house, which I took full use of. Because Mike, her husband at the time, made her smoke outside." But the cramped quarters provided a harsh introduction to the new reality Tomas faced. "He couldn't go upstairs, he couldn't go downstairs, he couldn't go anywhere," Roy McHugh recalled. "He had access to the living room, the kitchen, and that was it."

"I just kind of went into a shell and just shut up," said Tomas.

Brie soon moved in with Tomas and his family, with mixed results. It proved beneficial to the budding couple, since she was learning to become a caregiver, but it was also stressful. "I didn't want to do it," Young recalled, "because she would come home and say things like, 'Got all my bills paid today! Happy day!' and here's my mom and we're having trouble trying to pay the bills in this house, so she'd tell her to shut the fuck up."

In those early days, whenever Tomas and Brie ventured out, they went in Brie's car. "She would have to load me into the car and then take the chair and fold it and put it in the trunk," Tomas recalled. The process of transferring him from chair to car was awkward and difficult for anyone, let alone a small young woman like Brie. But the physical difficulties paled in comparison to the heavy emotional toll Tomas suffered when venturing out into society. "We were at the gas station right up there on the corner of Barry," he said, "and there was a guy parked behind us getting gas, and she was getting gas, and he saw me . . . and the window was up so I never heard him when he said, 'Honey, if I was your boyfriend, you wouldn't have to pump your own gas.' And she didn't know what to say, and I didn't hear him, and she didn't tell me about it right away. I was away from the situation or I would have said something."

Tomas's friend Roy McHugh also recalled getting out with him that summer, trying to break Young out of his shell. "I can remember going out with him places and stuff like that, and we used to like to drink beer a lot, and then he got to not wanting to drink beer, because he couldn't control when he had to pee. He had a leg bag on, and I'd help him into the bathroom and we'd prop his leg up on the toilet and then drain the bag, but then he'd have an accident and he couldn't control it and didn't want to do things that could provoke an accident.* He was conscious about it and everything else. It's a hard thing to live with—like, remember when you were twenty-four? I didn't know what I wanted to do with my life when I was twenty-four, but you had endless possibilities."

---

* These continued accidents eventually prompted him to make the switch to an internal catheter.

Young's reaction was to spend more time at home. "It made me more hesitant to go out in public," he said. "But I would still go out. Some nights I'd be fine, and we'd go out and wouldn't have any problems at all. Some nights, you can't win for losing. So it was a touch-and-go situation, and I didn't like going out much."

In addition to his new physical constraints, Tomas faced constant pain and leaned awkwardly in his chair to compensate. While he could sit up, he found it painful to maintain an upright position. "It hurts in my neck and it radiates to my shoulders and upper back," he said at the time. "It stops about chest level, where I'm paralyzed from."

Along with the time I spent at Tomas's bedside and speaking with those close to him, the book *Wheeling and Dealing: Living with Spinal Cord Injury* has been an indispensable resource in my quest to learn the nuances and complexities surrounding life with spinal cord injuries. In it, author Esther Isabelle Wilder cites chronic pain as "one of the most serious complications associated with SCI." She continues: "Many individuals with SCI have an unmet need for pain management. Individuals who sustained gunshot wounds are especially likely to experience chronic pain." Tomas's case, therefore, was not atypical.

At this early stage in his recovery, Tomas was taking carbamazepine, gabapentin, and morphine for pain, and was already having to increase his morphine dose in order for it to remain effective. This was in addition to his taking tizanidine anti-spasm medication, omeprazole for morning nausea, and the antidepressant bupropion (Wellbutrin). He was also taking the blood thinner warfarin to prevent blood clots, in addition to the vena cava filter surgically implanted into his abdomen.* Side effects from this daily cocktail included general grogginess, nausea, and constipation.

---

* The vena cava filter is a vascular filter device that is implanted in the inferior vena cava to trap blood clots traveling from the legs, preventing them from reaching the heart and lungs.

In addition to the prescription medications, Tomas also regularly smoked marijuana, which also helped lessen the muscle spasms and spasticity (tightness) Tomas experienced. "I used to have really bad problems with stomach spasms and leg spasms," he told me in 2013. "I would sleep at night and have my legs kick everywhere. Basically [Brie] had to sleep in a different bedroom."

Being paralyzed from the chest down also severely impaired his body's ability to control its own temperature through shivering or sweating in the paralyzed area. Another significant health issue Tomas faced was autonomic dysreflexia, or dangerously high blood pressure. Relatively common among patients with SCI similar to Tomas's, symptoms of autonomic dysreflexia can include sudden and excruciating headaches and blurred vision. This alarming spike in blood pressure is caused by painful stimuli emanating from below the level of the spinal cord injury—thus the patient does not feel the pain itself. Common causes are bladder distension, an impacted bowel, or other stimuli which would typically cause pain for an able-bodied individual. If not quickly addressed, this affliction can constitute a medical emergency.

In late 2005, Tomas suffered such an emergency and was rushed to the ER. "They put him on clonidine and that didn't do any good, so they put him on nitroglycerin gel," said Cathy. The gel is applied directly to the chest. "The scary thing about it with the spinal cord injury," she continued, "is that your blood pressure's so low anyway normally that his blood pressure will shoot up to like 200 over 140, and then if he takes clonidine or uses the nitroglycerin, it can bottom out at like 70 over 36. Just like that."

Yet another issue common to individuals with SCI is weight loss, due in large part to muscle atrophy. The loss of muscle between skin and bone can in turn lead to the skin breaking down over pressure points, causing pressure sores, which are "the single health problem that most often accompanies SCI," according to *Wheeling and Dealing.* As many as 85 percent of all individuals with

SCI battle pressure sores. These sores, which occur almost exclusively over bony prominences such as the hip bones, are caused by sustained pressure on a small area of soft tissue—most often from lying or sitting in one position for too long.

When I saw a photo by Eugene Richards of a shirtless Tomas from a 2006 article in the *Nation*, I noticed a dressing on Tomas's right hip. I asked him if it was a pressure sore. No, he explained—it was a cigarette burn. "That was because back then I had a very bad habit of smoking a cigarette and falling asleep, and the cigarette would invariably land somewhere on my body where I couldn't feel it," he said. "So it burned me."

Because of the pain, the physical limitations, and the psychological hardship of life after his injury, Tomas found himself gravitating toward the safe, simple pastime of watching baseball on TV. As the 2004 Major League Baseball regular season wound down that fall and the playoffs began, he rediscovered a love he'd developed as a child for the sport. "I didn't really play it a whole lot, but I gravitated toward it in the eighties because of Bo Jackson, George Brett, and whatnot," he recalled. Watching from the confines of his hospital bed behind his mother's couch, he witnessed the Boston Red Sox's fairytale ride to a World Series win. "While I'm laying here recovering from the gunshot wound," he said, "the Red Sox, after not having won a World Series in eighty-six years, after not beating the Yankees in the playoffs in so long, they came back from being down three-zero to finally beat the Yankees, and then they swept the Cardinals that year. And I became a fan of the Boston Red Sox."

There were visitors, too. Nathan visited whenever his Army schedule allowed it. "Every chance I could get a pass, I'd drive home, or . . . maybe on leave, I'd get to see him, but I didn't really get to see him much," he said. "I barely saw him, pretty much the whole time I was in the Army."

By Halloween 2004, within days of the conclusion of the Red Sox's unlikely ride to the World Series title, Tomas and Brie moved out of Cathy's house and into their own, a three-bedroom ranch in northern Kansas City. The home was built by local high-school students as part of a vo-tech program. Tomas paid for the home in part using a lump-sum financial award from the VA. By this time, he was also receiving monthly financial compensation from the VA as a retired soldier. He soon was provided with a handicapped-accessible van, which was replaced with a new model every couple of years. "I mean, he's not hurting for money," McHugh commented, putting things in perspective, "but you know, even if they were giving him a million dollars a month, it's still not enough money for what happened to him."

The new home afforded Tomas a new sense of freedom and independence following his experience the past few months in the cramped quarters of his mom's duplex. He could roll up the wheelchair ramp onto the front porch, through the front door, and throughout the house on the hardwood floors.

Despite this increased physical freedom, though, something was still missing. "When Tomas came home from rehab he was obviously focused on gaining as much independence as he could, but that doesn't give your life purpose," Brie said at the time. "And so he felt pretty useless for a long time. He didn't get out of bed, he played PlayStation, watched movies, listened to music, read magazines, and he would watch the news, listen to Bush and Rumsfeld and everyone and get so upset about all the lies that they were telling."

Or, as McHugh put it, "He didn't feel like doing anything." And the occasions when he did try something often ended in disappointment. "It's not like he was just lying in bed, depressed, but he would try things and it would set him back," McHugh recalled in 2013. "He called me up—and to this day I still try to say yes to everything he asks me to do—he called me up [in 2005] and was like, 'Hey man, the Warped Tour is coming to town, you wanna go?' And

I'm like, 'Sure,' so we bought tickets and I drove all the way out to pick him up, and we were driving out to the Warped Tour, we were there for—it was summer, too, so it was really hot—we were there less than an hour and had to leave. Really discouraging, you know, 'cause stuff's hard enough, and he can't even just do something as simple as sit at a concert. That stuff would get him down."

Tomas was adrift, lost in a life which he felt no longer had any meaning. He was caught in what Viktor Frankl, in his classic *Man's Search for Meaning*, called the "existential vacuum." "Suffering ceases to be suffering in some way at the moment it finds a meaning," Frankl wrote. "What man actually needs is not a tensionless state but rather the striving and struggling for a worthwhile goal, a freely chosen task." *Wheeling and Dealing* offers a similar sentiment in expressing the importance of having a goal or mission in the process of coming to terms with paralysis: "Sense of purpose is a powerful predictor of adjustment to SCI."

Tomas's Army buddy Riley Soden became a frequent visitor to the new home in early 2005, having moved back to Kansas City after his discharge from the military in February. He had attempted to contact Tomas earlier, but the Army told him that his friend was in a coma and denied him any of Tomas's family's contact information. "It was two or three days after I was back in Kansas City that I went out there and saw him for the first time," Soden recalled. He told local paper *Pitch Weekly* that that first visit "was really awkward. Not awkward in the sense of our friendship. I just hadn't seen him in the wheelchair or seen him with a disability. It really kind of hurt. . . . To help him move, it really gets to me sometimes. It breaks my heart to see him [injured] because he is such a good friend."

Soden visited Tomas's house on April 4, 2005, the first anniversary of Black Sunday. Tomas marked the occasion by burning his blood-soaked flak vest in a metal garbage can in his driveway, watching from his wheelchair alongside Soden as a cloud of thick black smoke wafted over the neighborhood. "It took a *lot* of lighter fluid," Tomas recalled. Exactly how he got the jacket back had been lost in the haze of his memory. Soden presented the most likely scenario—"I think somebody did inventory at Walter Reed or something and realized there was a bag with his name on it and had it sent to him."

"It had like a pin-sized hole, like a needle sized hole right here," Tomas said, pointing to his left collarbone, "and then there was nothing in the back of the vest, no hole. 'Cause by the time it had gone through me it had lost its oomph and just . . . stopped. I remember there were slits down the side of it, and apparently that was the result of US Army investigators looking for the round."

Burning the vest was a cathartic gesture. But the pain remained, the wheelchair remained, and an uncertain future loomed.

Chapter 7

Purpose

The way in which a man accepts his fate and all the suffering it entails, the way in which he takes up his cross, gives him ample opportunity—even under the most difficult circumstances—to add a deeper meaning to his life.

—Viktor Frankl, *Man's Search for Meaning*

Phil Donahue hadn't forgotten about Tomas Young. Months after the pair met at Walter Reed, Donahue was mulling over how to tell Tomas's story effectively. He and his wife, Marlo Thomas, had visited Young at the duplex in Liberty in the fall of 2004 and Donahue told Tomas that he wanted to write a book telling his story. Tomas said he was "shocked and pleasantly surprised about this suggestion, but still unclear about how I felt about everything. I was still new to my paralysis and quite emotionally and physically withdrawn."

About six months later, Donahue reconsidered, deciding to scrap the book and do a documentary film instead. "I thought, 'What the hell am I talking book here?'" he told the *New York Observer* in 2007. "I've spent my life in television. Let's do a movie."

A mutual friend, DeeDee Halleck, pointed Donahue toward a filmmaker named Ellen Spiro. A phone call from Donahue got the ball rolling, and the pair soon began to share mutual excitement about a possible film project. "I thought he was a crank caller," Spiro recalled with a laugh, "because to me, Phil Donahue was so famous he was almost like a fictional character, you know—he wasn't a real person. But he was very down to earth, and just was really operating off his own intuition that Tomas was this important person with an important story to tell, and we kind of just got working on that right away."

"She just bought this story cold," Donahue remembered. "And we both took chances, really, on each other. She didn't really know what kind of film guy [I was]—how am I to work with, all that. And I didn't have any real feel for her skill. So it turned out to be the first break of the movie for me, because she turned out to be fabulous. A wonderful filmmaker."

Donahue also needed to spend more time getting to know Tomas, about whom he knew little, aside from the fact that he was a horribly injured soldier. "When I went to visit him in Kansas City after the Walter Reed experience, I had no idea what his politics were," Donahue said. "If he wanted to go back to Iraq, that's the movie I would have made. But as I sat in his living room when we went out to see him, I noticed on the coffee table there were bumper stickers. And one of the bumper stickers said 'Draft Republicans.' And that was my first indication . . . what I had here was a warrior turned anti-warrior."

Donahue also found Tomas to be in possession of a sharp intellect. "He's a bright light," he said. "The Army recognized that immediately. Tomas has a brain." Add to this the fact that Young had been particularly attentive to political matters and current events from an early age, and it added another layer to the story. "Before I joined the military I was politically minded, but not necessarily politically active," Tomas said. "I only became politically active once I had joined an organization called Iraq Veterans Against the War." The film picks up the story just as Tomas had begun to make that transition.

"I guess it all started when I went to my friend's house and watched *Fahrenheit 9/11*," Tomas recalled. The documentary, directed by Michael Moore, had hit US theaters just a couple of weeks before Tomas was released from VA care in Saint Louis. The DVD release was that fall. While Young recalled that he was "smoking pot at the time and that makes you very emotional," he was sufficiently invested in the storyline—the 9/11 attacks and the war in Iraq—to be brought to tears without any help. "I watched all this stuff . . . and I just started crying, I was like 'It's not right,'" he said. "That was when I decided . . . my mom was part of a group—Military Families Speak Out, MFSO, and they knew of a group called IVAW, Iraq Veterans Against the War, and so I joined up with them. Then Phil came and visited me and presented the idea of making a documentary movie about what I went through, and I didn't really—even though I should have—I didn't consider the fact that it was my first year of recovery, and I was going to be doing all this."

Young's drive to share his story, which eclipsed what should have been the priority—his health and recovery—was simply a continuation of his objection to the war in the first place. He'd objected to war in Iraq as soon as it became a possibility. The catastrophic injury strengthened the basis of his objections while simultaneously providing him a platform from which to speak out.

Donahue and Spiro pitched the film project to Tomas during a visit to his home around May 2005. "I said, 'Tomas, I want to do a film that makes a statement—I want to make a political statement—and I can't do it without you, without your permission,'" Donahue recalled. "'I want to see this pain up close.'" Tomas felt the time was right and agreed. "I became clearer that I was injured in an improper war and felt I needed to speak out," he said. "So I saw the film as not just focusing on my recovery process, but also about my new activism that was just in the beginning stages."

Spiro was struck during that first meeting by Tomas's humility. "I think the main gist was like, 'Yeah I'd be happy to work with you, but you know, what do I have to say?'" she said. "And, obviously, when he started speaking he had got a lot to say, and I think that humility was part of what made him such a strong character. He really could have been anybody's son or anybody's brother, caught in that situation. And that he was somebody that came back, being as close to death on the battlefield as you could be but still being able to tell his story, I think is what brought people in."

Tomas's sense of humor also resonated with Spiro. "I thought he had the most important quality for making an engaging story about a serious social issue, and that was that he was funny," she recalled. "And it didn't matter—all the hardships that he'd been through and were still to come, he just had a way of laughing in the face of all this stuff that was very, I think, empowering for him, and part of what made him such a lovable person."

Within weeks of that initial meeting, filming began. Ellen preferred to work alone, using just a unipod, to create an intimate, unstaged atmosphere. She stayed at Young's house during filming, which further established an emotional connection. "Tomas was generous enough to let me use his guest room," Spiro said, "and I would just stay there, spending most of my time not filming—actually, that's just how I've always made my films: I just spend a lot of time with people, and then when the time was right and it seemed appropriate, that's when I filmed."

Spiro's steady presence in the Young household also helped Tomas become more comfortable and open during filming. "He got used to me being around, just like, 'Oh, there goes Ellen again,'" Spiro said with a laugh. "But we developed a rapport and a friendship and I think the more he got to know me and the more he got to know Phil, I think it was pretty obvious that we were on his side, you know . . . that it was just his story, and we wanted that to unfold in the most honest way possible."

Still, it took Tomas a little while to open up. "Initially, I was a bit mindful of the cameras," he said in 2008, "but eventually it got to the point where it dawned on me that the more people see the day-to-day workings of my life—talking to my ex-wife about my erectile issues and my blood thinners—that's very personal, heady stuff; having my mom stick the catheter in inside the van. These are all very intense things to watch, I'm sure, but the more people saw about my daily life the more they'd know, one, not to make impetuous decisions, and two, this war has personal consequences and ramifications that aren't shown on the nightly news."

An early focus of filming was the wedding of Tomas and Brie, which took place in August 2005. "[Brie] basically had been planning her wedding since high school," Tomas recalled. "She had this whole thing planned out—she had a signature drink for the wedding, she had daisies, and . . . we almost had to wear yellow cummerbunds," he recalled disdainfully. In a move designed to assume a modicum of control, Tomas declared that he would choose the music. "And so I compiled four CDs of . . . crazy stuff, and she told me the first CD had to be lyrically tame and kind of quiet because that was when her older relatives were going to be there, and that it could get harder as the evening progressed. The first one, first track was Jimi Hendrix's version of the 'Star-Spangled Banner.' My brother Nathan was in his class A uniform, and so he started saluting because it was the national anthem, and . . . it goes on for a *long* time. . . . All the old people at the wedding were apparently wondering, 'What the hell was *that*?'" he recalled with a satisfied smile.

The rehearsal dinner the night before the wedding came to an abrupt end, a development which Tomas in retrospect viewed as an omen. "I should have known it was something bad in the wind," he said. "There was a bad storm coming and two houses down there was a domestic dispute that ended with gunfire, and so the police came and told us all to go back into our house."

Cathy had cut the back pockets out of his military uniform for the occasion, but Tomas decided to wear a tux on his wedding day. He fretted about soiling it by having a bowel accident during the ceremony. Brie wore a classic white wedding dress. The ceremony took place in a marquee in Cathy's backyard, muddy from the previous night's storm. Roy McHugh and Riley Soden were among the groomsmen. "The ground is so wet and saturated and muddy that we had to put pieces of plywood down to act as the altar and the aisle," Tomas recalled, "and as we're rolling back down the aisle as husband and wife . . . because her dress is so big, it gets caught up in my wheel of my chair, and my chair goes off into the side, and I have to ask her family members to come and help lift the chair back up onto the aisle."

During the reception, Nathan stepped up, introduced himself as Tomas's "little brother" and explained how the pair had been through a lot together before welcoming Brie to the family and proposing a toast to the new couple. Brimming with pride, youngest brother Timmy then spoke: "I'd like to say something: I'm *proud* of my brother Tomas for going in the Army and being *brave*, and going in Iraq."

Soon after their wedding, Tomas and Brie, along with a cameraman and a lighting tech, took the van to Texas for their "honeymoon." The first stop was Fort Hood, Tomas's old Army base. The film crew lifted Young's wheelchair up the steps so he could access the staff offices of 2-5 Cav. "I went and asked the sitting first sergeant in my company why we were sent out on such a poorly planned mission," Tomas recalled, "and he kind of stammered, didn't give me an answer." It wasn't long until word of Young's unwanted presence was broadcast to the authorities. "I had received a call from one of my buddies that I was in with that was still there at Fort Hood, and he wanted to meet me and catch up with me," Young said, "so I went to the parking lot of the sports restaurant that was on base, and he showed up and told me that there were MPs [military police] coming to get me, so I'd better hurry up and get off the base." He hurriedly departed, never to return.

Young's subsequent visit to Camp Casey proved more fruitful. He arrived at the camp, set up by activist Cindy Sheehan in Crawford,

Texas, to coincide with President Bush's vacation there on August 28, a punishing 110-degree day. Sheehan, whose son Casey had died in the fighting on Black Sunday in Sadr City, established the camp in an effort to publicize her wish to meet with President Bush to ask him why her son had died. It quickly become a focus of antiwar activism. There were tents set up with tables and a podium for speakers, who that day included former State Department official Ann Wright and actor Martin Sheen. A field of nearly two thousand crosses, decorated with flowers, boots, and flags, stood outside to represent those who didn't come home from Iraq. Tomas wore a special cooling vest that had pockets for frozen gel inserts. "Because it was so hot down there I had to, every three or four hours, take the gel packs out and put them in an ice box or however they did it, and sit in my car for two hours with the air conditioning cranked full blast," he recalled. "It took a lot out of me." But Tomas, wearing a star-spangled bandanna, stayed the course, meeting people, posing for photographs, conducting interview after interview, passionately pushing his pro-veteran, antiwar message to anyone who would listen. Young told the gathered press he also would like to meet with the president: "I feel he owes me an explanation as to why a soldier can volunteer to go over and fight for his country and lose his ability to walk, plus a lot of other important functions, and why I am not worth the funding for stem-cell research."

Not surprisingly, the meeting with President Bush never materialized. However, it was as a result of his trip to Camp Casey that Tomas's life took yet another turn. He discovered that he possessed a powerful voice, facilitated by his intelligence, openness, and political bent and authenticated by the devastating price he had paid on the battlefield. People listened to him. His desire to speak out against the war and to advocate for veterans' issues only deepened with each passing week.

"Camp Casey, from my point of view, was an incredible experience for him because he met so many other people that were on the same page with their thoughts," Ellen Spiro observed. "Before that, he just seemed very isolated in, you know—his little world, and it was hard to see . . . and this connected him to the bigger picture, so I don't know if he would have gone there had we not been making the film, but once we got there, it was clear that he was on a roll, so to speak."

"Tomas was always politically minded," Roy McHugh remembered, "like he'd watch the news and do all sorts of stuff that you wouldn't think a normal seventeen-year-old kid would be into, that wasn't, like, Mr. Academic. He'd always be into politics." In addition, it wasn't in Tomas's nature to shy away from sharing the embarrassing and painful details of his daily life as an injured veteran. "Tomas has always been an outgoing and personable person," McHugh said. "And he's been really open about what's been going on with him. I wouldn't want to talk to anybody about it." Neither would most people. Tomas chose not to withdraw and suffer in silence—a natural human reaction to catastrophic injury—but to speak out.

It certainly didn't hurt that activism and speaking out were in Tomas's blood: Cathy, too, had developed an activist streak early on. "I was certainly not a hippie—I was upper middle class, white, but I was born in the sixties, so I was in high school at the height of activism," she said. "We had a sit-in at my school to improve the cafeteria food." It didn't help, she remembered. But her penchant for speaking out remained and was imparted to her son.

"I had always been kind of a liberal-minded person, ever since I was a little kid," said Tomas. "Mom tells me stories about how we would go to the abortion clinic on Saturdays where they would have a pro-life demonstration, and we would go to the local laundromat and buy wire coat hangers and throw the coat hangers at the protest demonstrators and say, 'Do you want to go back to this? Is this what you want to go back to?' I was maybe nine, ten years old."

As a child, Tomas Young developed what blossomed into a lifelong passion for comic books. This passion was such that, as a fifth-grader, he shoplifted a couple of comics from a local drug store and ran out into the street—where he was hit by an oncoming car. "I guess if you believe in karma, that was my karmic payback," he said. He sustained significant injuries and was hospitalized for several days. Young was particularly enamored with the comic-book characters Batman and the Punisher "because," he explained, "they're just regular guys that—they weren't born on any [faraway] planet, or bitten by a radioactive spider, or any of that—they were just regular guys who had horrible things happen to them in both cases. In the Punisher's case, his wife and child were killed, and in Batman's case, his parents were killed. They wanted to make sure nobody else went through what they went through."

When I pointed out the parallel between the driving motivation of Tomas's comic-book heroes and his own drive to share his message in the hopes that other soldiers wouldn't meet the same horrible fate as he, he simply gave a shrug and said, "Yeah, well, I guess."

Young's newfound political activism also provided the meaning and purpose he so desperately needed in his life. This purpose served to reinvigorate Tomas—a critical step in the still newly injured soldier's path to recovery. "It was a new light and a new push for him, and it definitely helped his character at the time," Riley Soden observed. "Tomas becoming an activist and being motivated about this thing . . . it did give him a purpose and some pride in something in his life where he did kind of feel useless at one point, but I think once he realized that he had the ability to touch people in a different way, that he really shined to it."

Young approached his new role with sufficient vigor and commitment that he actually limited his intake of medications that were robbing him of the mental clarity he needed in order to speak out effectively. "When we met Tomas he wasn't very articulate," Spiro told broadcaster Bill Moyers in 2008. "He was pretty much addicted to morphine, and with his own willpower started to wean himself from the morphine because he knew he wasn't going to be an effective voice if he couldn't form a sentence." Spiro later told me that Tomas became "increasingly clearer as the process went on. He was on so many drugs that, you know, I couldn't even count them all, but I knew he was weaning himself off the ones that made him more foggy."

The months immediately following Camp Casey were a blur of public appearances for Tomas, from peace vigils to antiwar rallies to speaking at churches and appearing on national television. All the while, Ellen Spiro's camera was rolling. It captured Brie laboring to wheel Tomas through the grass at a rally in Washington, D.C., where his mother was moved to tears at a display of photographs of the dead organized in a chain. "You could have been there," Cathy said, hugging her son. "It really is overwhelming."

Spiro captured another especially touching moment that day, between Tomas and the young widow of an Iraq war vet. "Tomas brought a lot of innate insight and talent, and also courage and stamina," said Donahue. He added that the scene still brings him to tears.

> It's where they roll Tomas up to a rope, behind which are Gold Star Mothers and people who've lost loved ones to the war. Husbands, brothers, sons, daughters, and they're standing there holding pictures of their loved ones who came home in a pine box. One woman—and it's clearly her husband, they're young, they could be late twenties—she's holding up a picture of her husband in uniform and they roll Tomas up, and they all lean over the rope and touch him, they stroke his cheek and they lean over the rope to kiss him, and Tomas leans forward to give them his cheek. Because he knows that, for a vicarious moment, they are allowing themselves to believe that they are touching and kissing the loved one that they will never kiss again. He was there in the same war and somehow he became, in that moment, a surrogate. A touch that was alive, not the touch of the photograph that they're holding . . . and here he is, twenty-five years old at the time, and he has the insight to know and to offer himself to them so they can have this moment. Oh, you know . . . I mean, it just takes my breath away.

"It was . . . indescribable," Tomas said of the scene during an interview with the *Today Show* in 2008. "If I, by allowing a mother, or a wife of somebody who didn't come home, to touch my face, to feel some connection with me, for whatever reason, then I'm more than happy to step into that role because they need somebody to help turn to, to touch, to do whatever they need to let go of their grief. I'm more than happy to help with that."

Spiro's camera was there in September 2005 when Tomas—not long after he'd been rushed to the ER during his scary episode of autonomic dysreflexia—met Bobby Muller, a US Marine Corps veteran and a staunch advocate for veterans' rights and peace, who had been shot and paralyzed in 1969 in Vietnam, suffering an injury similar to Tomas's. Muller was incredulous when he learned of Tomas's short period of post-injury care. "You got short shrift," Muller told Young, adding, nearly forty years after his injury, "I think I'm in better condition than you are." Muller had stayed in the hospital for a full year after his injury and received an additional nine months of outpatient care upon his return home, dwarfing the care Tomas received, barely more than three months. "Again, I'm just going to say it, I think you got short shrift, man. You've seen the squandering of billions of dollars for a bullshit war destroying people, you get shot, and now they're gonna *skimp* on giving you the kind of treatment and care that you obviously have a right to and deserve? I got to the point where I said, 'OK, here it is. If I don't fight this system, I will die.' You got every right in the world to say this is bullshit. What are they gonna do to you?"

In November, a month after Tomas attended a vigil in downtown Kansas City to mark the somber news that the US military death count in Iraq had reached two thousand, Spiro joined Young and his mother in the van as they headed for Fort Campbell, Kentucky. Tomas's brother Nathan was preparing to ship out to Iraq with the 101st Airborne Division.

Tomas's younger brother could have opted out of his deployment, Cathy recalled. "There was always the option that you can go through the paperwork and have your second not go because your first was injured," she said. "But it was something he wanted to do, you know—he felt like he had to do it, it was his duty, so that's always what it was for him."

Nathan, whose political beliefs run further to the right than Tomas's, didn't object to the war in Iraq, a perspective which didn't change after two long and arduous tours of duty in the country. But he also respected his older brother's antiwar stance. "The way I see it is, if somebody's allowed to have that point of view, it's definitely somebody that's been injured in war," Nathan said. "Somebody that can speak out against the war, I mean, the only person that has a leg to stand on on that, no pun intended, would be Tomas. Just because he served his country and didn't go AWOL like some other people. . . . He didn't agree with it but he still had his orders."

That night, a tearful Cathy and a stoic Tomas bid farewell to Nathan. "Nathan has always, in every situation he's been in, thought he was ten feet tall and bulletproof," Tomas said in the film. "I'm scared—I know what can happen. . . . I couldn't let him see that, because that was the time for him to have his mom cry and be scared over him. I couldn't let him, the guy that he looks up to so much, see that *he* was scared."

As at Fort Hood, Spiro didn't have permission to film that day, but one of the film's producers, working with Nathan, approached each of the soldiers who were filmed. All gave their permission. "If [they] hadn't, then we wouldn't have been able to use any of that stuff," said Spiro, "and it was some of the most—it was definitely like a really amazing scene that day where soldiers were leaving and especially from Cathy's perspective, you know—one son comes back paralyzed and the other one goes off to war. It's unbelievable that anybody could go through all that."

Following Nathan's deployment, Cathy said, "I felt like I didn't breathe for twelve months. Every time the phone would ring, I would be just. . . . The first time, when I got the call about Tomas, it had never occurred to me that anything would happen. You know, I had never even—it never crossed my mind that I would get that phone call. And when Nathan left, *every day* I thought I was going to get that phone call. I waited for it every day." Every day she checked the website icasualties.org to monitor the numbers of US and Iraqi dead and wounded—and to see if Nathan was among them.

The toll on Tomas was sometimes unbearable, too. Still coming to terms with life as a paraplegic, he endured bouts of frustration and depression. The grief and sorrow overtook him at times. "There are a lot of times that I sit back there in my back bedroom, lying in bed and just . . . crying. With very little control," he said. "It usually happens after my body does something to show how much it disagrees with me. It happens sometimes when I watch people walk down the street. I'm jealous of people that can walk."

In December, Tomas visited New York, his first stop being an appearance at the Lafayette Avenue Presbyterian Church in Brooklyn. Despite his arriving about ninety minutes late due to gridlock caused by a transit workers' strike, "the place was still packed," Tomas recalled. "So I started giving the speech, and because it was being filmed for the movie, there were lights everywhere, and I had on a sweater, and so I became very hot and had to take off the sweater, and bend over the knees because I would get dizzy."

Young's talk focused on how President Bush had promised to exact revenge and "got everyone excited, and *I* was excited, wanted to go to Afghanistan and get the people that did this to us." The rush to war in Iraq, he said, may have been a departure from the Christian values Bush publicly held so dear. "I'm concerned that President Bush was trying to use Jesus Christ as an advocate for the war," Tomas said in the church that evening. "But I always remembered—at least from the Bible that *I* read, Jesus Christ was always about peaceful things and love, and whatsoever you do unto the least of my brothers you do unto me, and I . . . it just shocks me that a man who tries to live his life by such devout Christian philosophies seems to skew so much on this one issue."

It was a powerful moment—with more than a touch of irony, given that Tomas, an atheist, was delivering a speech referencing biblical values in a church. But it worked. The crowd gave Tomas a standing ovation. Pained at the attention, he grimaced slightly and waved them off, humble as always.

While in New York, Tomas also stopped by the *60 Minutes* studios. The resulting episode, "Wounds of War," which aired the following February, profiled five wounded veterans and their postwar lives. Tomas was surprised to find that he was the only wounded vet who spoke out against the war. "It felt like a Trident chewing-gum commercial," he said later. "It was like, 'Four out of five vets support war over peace.'" He was also surprised when the network edited out his complaints about his unit's poor leadership.

In December, he headed south to participate in a conference in Miami called Vets4Vets. "It was some flimflam operation set up by this psychiatrist who promises that he can heal the warrior's wounded mind," said Tomas, who attended as a participant, not a speaker. "At the end of the day," Tomas recalled, "they said, 'All right, you can go check out Miami.' I'm like, 'Sweet, where can we go?'" Their options were limited to a short strip—"They said, 'You see where that restaurant is? To where *that* restaurant is,'" Tomas recalled—or the beach, which is one of the more wheelchair-unfriendly locales imaginable. Tomas went to the hotel bar.

Less than a year into filming *Body of War* and not even ten months after their wedding, Tomas and Brie's relationship was strained and in serious trouble. The odds had been firmly stacked against them from the very beginning, the main liabilities being their youth, their limited life experience, and the fact that their relationship had consisted of just one date before Tomas's deployment and subsequent paralysis. Adjusting to married life is hard enough for most young couples without adding a catastrophic injury to the equation.

Brie intimated at the time that a key contributor was the blurred line between her roles as both wife and caregiver. "Sometimes," she said, Tomas "gets angry and says we're basically roommates, and that I'm his housekeeper and his maid." Plus she pointed out that they were around each other "a lot, which kind of works on each other's nerves."

Any hope for sexual intimacy between the newlyweds had quickly faded too. The young couple's sex life was practically nonexistent. Tomas's spinal cord injury meant that any attempts at sexual activity required extensive preparation, thus robbing the moment of any spontaneity. He told Bobby Muller that he'd tried Viagra and it had worked a couple of times, but then stopped working. Other supposed remedies involved pumps (Brie said in the film that because of Tomas's external catheter and blood thinners, the pump would "make his penis bleed, which freaks him out") or direct injections into the penis. They didn't work.

Tomas was also suspicious of Brie's relationship with an ex-boyfriend, with whom she worked at a local comedy club. "They worked the same shift, the evening shift, and she would pick him up and go to work," he recalled, adding that her time spent away from home began to increase. "I got tired of it. . . . All I could do was make my own inferences, so I decided I didn't want to be with her."

Meanwhile, the cameras were still rolling. "I was like, do I want the movie to include the divorce?" Tomas recalled. "So I probably would have asked for it sooner, but I was worried about how it would look in the movie. And finally I just couldn't take it anymore, and so I rolled out and she was watching a DVRed episode of *CSI: Miami*. And I said, 'Can we have a talk?' And she said 'Now?' And I said 'Yes, now.' And so she—sigh—paused the movie and joined me over at the table." Tomas recalled that when he and Brie began discussing their relationship, the damage was readily apparent. "I said, 'I think we should get separated.' And I don't know, maybe I'm a folksy, old-fashioned guy, but when your spouse asks you if you should get separated, the likely response should be 'Well, what can we do to fix this?,' not, 'OK—I'll pack some stuff and go spend the night at my friend's house and I'll pick the rest of my stuff up in a few days.' And when she came to pick her stuff up she came with her mom, who looked at me with hateful looks, and I'm like, OK. And she called me like three or four days later and said, 'Are we going to just do a trial separation and get back together or are we going to get a divorce,'cause if we're just going to stay separated then you need to pay for my apartment that I just signed the lease on for a year.' So I said, 'Well, I guess we're getting a divorce.'"

Tomas's second wife Claudia was present during our conversation about his first marriage. She asked, "Did you have a bad feeling on your wedding night?" To which Tomas responded in the affirmative: "Mmm-hmmm. But I was scared. I was scared of being alone and not being able to take care of myself, or having to have my mom constantly around me. I didn't want either of those things, and I was scared that that was what was going to happen."

By June 2006, Brie had moved into her own apartment. After she left, Tomas removed the framed wedding portrait, taken by Phil Donahue, from the wall and put it in the closet. He also put his framed flag and Purple Heart citations away. "I don't really understand why they give you an award for getting shot, but they do," Tomas said in the film. "My wife liked to have these kinds of things up on display. Like this machine-autographed certificate of appreciation from our president. I already know I got shot. I have an everyday reminder of it. I don't need to come out here to my living room and see a flag and a Purple Heart to tell me what situation I'm in."

Chapter 8

A Glimmer of Hope

Throughout this whole experience, Tomas has wanted to live. He has come back from everything.

—Phil Donahue

It's May 19, 2013, and I'm back in Kansas City. Tomas called me this morning shortly before the scheduled start of our interview and asked if he could delay it by an hour or so. He'd suffered a particularly severe case of nausea and wanted a little more time to recover before we started. I arrive around noon, a little later than planned, on a cool, rainy Sunday. Tomas is reclined on his bed, wearing his "Reality Doesn't Give a Damn about Your Beliefs" T-shirt, his response to those who have recently been trying to impart their religious beliefs on him. As I sit to begin talking to him, Tomas asks Claudia to press the button on the vaporizer and give him a cigarette.

I figure our time together will be limited, so I get straight down to business. I ask him how the reunion went with Staff Sergeant Miltenberger and the other soldiers from his unit. "I canceled that because I had gotten tired of the media and putting on a face," he says, over the hum of the vaporizer. He explains that another factor in pulling out of the scheduled reunion was that he barely knew the other two participants. "These were the two guys who instigated this whole thing," he says. "They found out that I was doing an interview with Martha Raddatz and they called and said they were part of the same unit and wanted to do a reunion. I would do it just with Staff Sergeant Miltenberger, because he's the one who essentially saved me, but the other two, I felt they were just doing it to get their names out there, so I didn't want to do it with them."

The vaporizer bag is now full. Claudia removes it from the machine and passes it to Tomas, who inhales the marijuana vapor from it every few sentences, rustling the bag, as we talk.

Garett Reppenhagen walks in. Garett was here last time too, with his IVAW companions. He tells me that one of them, Kelly, in the latter stages of pregnancy when I met her last month, recently gave birth to a daughter. Garett sticks around, sitting on a bench on the opposite side of the bed, as I continue asking questions. I ask Tomas if he had followed through on his plan to stop granting interview requests after his anniversary. "Yeah. . . . The only thing I've done is *Huffington Post Live* and the Skype-in to the Bush library when they screened my film there, so all I've done since then were things that I was booked to do prior to April 20."*

When I ask if he's been getting some peace and quiet, Tomas said, "Trying to, yeah." He adds, "About three weeks ago I got asked on Twitter by a guy that hosts a podcast called *Revelations Radio* for my email address so listeners could send me well wishes. Well, I didn't realize that every email I got was going to be a call to accept Christ and follow him, and so I said, tell all of the *Revelations Radio* listeners I will not respond to any more emails." I tell Tomas I saw his tweet stating that he'd soon be shutting down his email address

---

* Tomas appeared via Skype at a screening of *Body of War* at the Angelika Film Center in Dallas on April 24, the evening before the dedication of the Bush Presidential Center in the same city.

due to the volume of proselytizing emails generated by the podcast. "Yeah, I said I was, but I didn't," Tomas says, adding with his trademark deadpan stare, "I lied to Christians."

"You're going to hell," Garett interjects with a grin.

When I ask Tomas if any other significant events have transpired since my last visit, he mentions that Brie, his ex-wife, had visited. "She had been emailing this morning radio show host to get her to call me," Tomas begins. "And so I finally called my ex-wife to get her to stop bothering this radio show host, and Claudia said ask her over. I didn't want to, because I didn't think she'd say yes, but I asked her and she said she'd love to. So she came by with her husband and talked for a few minutes. And then Claudia took her husband out of the room so it was just her and I." Tomas explains that Brie wanted to set the record straight about their ugly and clearly still painful mid-divorce financial battle. I opine that perhaps Brie had paid this recent visit in an effort to clear her conscience. "Yeah, I guess," Tomas responds. "So I forgave her, as the rules of a polite society dictate, and sent her on her way."

I ask if Tomas's family has visited—last time I was here, he had mentioned that his brother and grandparents were going to visit. "Yeah, they have been, yeah," is all he offers. Before I can follow up, the conversation shifts to the elephant in the room: Tomas advises me that the timeline he'd previously established (and already lengthened) for ending his life has changed again.

"Well, I made the decision around the beginning of April, when opening day happened, that I was going to miss baseball really bad so I wanted to stick around for one more season of baseball," he explains unconvincingly. He's happy to see his local team, the Kansas City Royals, atop the American League Central. "I said that I wasn't going to do, like any life-ending steps until after the end of the World Series. And then I told *Huffington Post Live* . . . if it becomes too unbearable, then I will take the steps to end my life. So right now it has no date—I'm just going to ride it out until it becomes too unbearable for me," he said, adding a more plausible explanation than the baseball excuse, "because I want to spend as much time as possible with my wife."

Tomas delivers the news of this momentous development as matter-of-factly as he'd provided the other updates, but the change is tangible: The pall that hung over this house back in April at the time of my first visit has lifted significantly. Tomas is once again beginning to focus on living instead of dying, something which, at least to me, was unthinkable just a few weeks ago. Later, when I ask Claudia to reflect on his change in perspective she says:

> I think as he stabilized the pain, I think he realized—'cause I think before you go further in, you think you can't handle it, and I guess like every day you handle it a little bit—so, you know. To feel like we were going to have to actually say goodbye was really freaky. . . . Once we got close to the anniversary, we're like—oh, I would miss a lot of things about you, or us, or the things you said, and so we got closer and closer. Which from an emotional . . . I mean . . . I thought I'd hit as deep as I could go until I went deeper. Every time. Every day I feel like I'm tired, I'm not sure if I can go on, you know, "How can I feel more than I feel in this very moment," and I end up feeling more and going deeper and noticing details about every hair coming out of every pore in his face, or I can see something different about an eyebrow, or an eyelash, or . . . that kind of level of detail that you never notice, 'cause you realize time is . . . and then we realized, well, if he feels he can bear it and he feels like he would miss me and if he wants to stay, and that's what he wants, then I'll go with him as far as he wants to go.

Eddie Vedder is also pleased to hear of his friend's decision. "I think I was in South America when he decided to, you know—pull the plug, and kind of set a date," he says. "I think that was really empowering—it was a beautiful and powerful response to his situation, and it allowed him to have some control. Here's a guy who had to be afforded some level of empowerment, and he had earned that. And I think it was liberating to the point where it made him feel so much better that he decided, well, in this situation, I can live a little bit longer."

Another positive development is that Tomas has only had to visit the hospital once since my last visit, for a clot in the IV port implanted in his chest. He went to the infusion clinic at the VA and they injected a blood thinner, which took care of it. But how long this can continue before Tomas reaches his stated threshold of unbearable pain is anyone's guess. He tells me that the Dilaudid dose has recently been increased to 9 milliliters an hour to keep the pain at bay.

Tomas asks Claudia for a cigarette and to turn on the vaporizer. She obliges. I ask Tomas and Garett how they first met. "The film, I think," Garett responds, then Tomas interjects: "Yeah, you worked for Bobby Muller at the time." Turning to me, he adds, indicating Garett, "He was the gateway to get to Bobby Muller."

Garett then began discussing Muller's recent struggles managing his pain and his medication regimen. He shares his plans to meet Muller soon. "I think most people think that veterans come home and they instantly start healing, they don't realize that those injuries can degrade and become more problems further down the road," Garett says. "And guys like Ron Kovic and Bobby Muller that have those spinal injuries, you know—you don't just recover from that."

"Yeah, I'm well aware," Tomas responds dryly.

"Oh, you are?" offers Garett, feigning surprise.

I interject that I recently reread Kovic's harrowing *Born on the Fourth of July*, and point out that the book was my first real introduction to the complexity and nature of SCI. "Yeah, I think every spinal injury is different," Garett says. Tomas thinks on this for a few seconds before adding, "Before I got shot and paralyzed from the chest down, I didn't know you could *get* paralyzed from the chest down. I thought it was just fully quadriplegic or paralyzed from the *waist* down."

As if by necessity, Garett, Claudia, and Tomas move to lighter matters, namely the scene in *Body of War* where Tomas and Garett wait at a curb and discuss the volleyball scene in *Top Gun*. In the scene, Garett says he and his fellow soldiers reenacted the volleyball scene in Kosovo, while Tomas laughs and adds that his unit did the same thing in Iraq.

"You want to know the truth?" Tomas says. "I was just talking shit, 'cause I hate that movie. I've never actually seen the movie."

Claudia, Garett, and I erupt into laughter. "*WHAAAT?*"

"Dude, I've seen the movie like fifty times 'cause it's hilarious," Garett says.

"You reenacted that scene! How did you do it?" Claudia asks.

"Because that scene is famous!" Tomas responds, before admitting, "Well, actually I may have seen it once when I was very young. 'Cause I remember more scenes than that one. I remember Goose, and I remember the Righteous Brothers scene . . . so I had to have seen it, but I never want to see it again."

As the momentum of the conversation begins to wane, I look down at my notes and fire off a question. Tomas's friend Riley had received his Purple Heart from George W. Bush; I ask Tomas if he remembered getting his. "Yeah—I was doing rehab at Jefferson Barracks in Saint Louis, and I had two master sergeants from Fort Hood, from my battalion's rear detachment unit, come and give me my two Purple Hearts."

When I respond that Tomas didn't exactly get the same kind of firepower that Riley got, he agrees and adds, "Well, that was because he was in Texas and it was Easter, so Dubya was on a goodwill photo-op at the Army hospital that Riley was at. And that morning, Riley was given double the amount of pain medications they normally gave him, and he goes, 'What's this?' and they go, 'It's because the president's coming.' So, you know . . . if you're all doped up, you're not necessarily going to find yourself in a position where you can cogently ask him why he would do it." Soden said he did, however, manage to ask President Bush whether he was sent to war "so we can have cheaper gas prices," but the pain meds had blurred his memory as to Bush's response, if any.

I tell Tomas that I saw one of his Purple Heart certificates down in the basement (he has two: one for each injury). I ask if he still has the medals. He nods and asks Claudia to get them. While she's gone, he says, "Claudia has one which she wears as a necklace, and when my brother and his wife and my niece come up, I think I'm going to give Aleksus [Tomas's niece] the other Purple Heart when she comes up next time."

Claudia returns with the awards, still in their presentation boxes. She takes them out and shows them to me. One has the ribbon removed, replaced with red silk thread to make a necklace. The other remains intact.

Tomas is tired and still a little nauseated at the end of our talk. He closes his eyes and sleeps.

Today isn't a typical day. A special event dubbed "A Tribute to Tomas Young" will take place tonight in a theater in downtown Kansas City. Phil Donahue and Tom Morello are behind the event, which was arranged as a show of support in response to the news of Young's decision to end his life. Tomas was to attend, but ultimately declined for a couple of reasons. Claudia had scouted the venue the previous day and determined that there were no exit doors on the floor up front, which meant that Tomas would have had to be carried down the steps all the way from the top of the house to the bottom in his very heavy electric wheelchair. This alone made Tomas anxious and hesitant about making the trip, but the nausea he suffered this morning convinced him not to attend.

Leaving Tomas to rest, I head downtown to the theater for tonight's event. I arrive during a pre-show meeting around a table in the theater's mezzanine that includes Morello, Donahue, and several others. The animated Morello, in his trademark baseball cap and sipping a glass of tea, is running through the plan for the evening. Donahue is no-nonsense but warm, unassuming, with gray hair and glasses. He's wearing jeans and a checked shirt, a "NO DRONES" button pinned to the collar of his leather jacket. I tell him that I overheard Morello saying during the meeting that tonight's show was Phil's idea. "Well . . . I don't know if it was my idea," he responds, "but I certainly wanted to do this. [Morello's] name came up, the discussion was under way and he called me. And you know, we had to figure out a venue." Donahue looks around. "This will be the biggest theater crowd that's ever seen our movie . . . but Tomas's condition is so severe, he can't even make it for this, and it's in the same city. So it gives you an idea of what he's going through."

About an hour later, Tom Morello takes the small stage set up at the foot of the movie screen and explains the plan for the evening to the packed house.

After the screening of *Body of War*, the music began, with opening acts Jacob George and Ike Reilly. George is a three-tour veteran of Afghanistan with PTSD who is in the midst of a bicycle ride across the nation, a ride he says won't be complete until the war is over. Reilly is a singer-songwriter who hails from Morello's hometown of Libertyville, Illinois.

I didn't know what to expect from Morello, who had warned us during the introduction that he was going to "rock [our] asses off." He began with the subdued "Battle Hymns," but the intensity ratcheted up with the more up-tempo "Flesh Shapes the Day." His stomping during this song shook the tiny stage violently, knocking his harmonica from the top of his Marshall amp and nearly sending his glass of Jameson whiskey off the stool it was perched on.

Morello turned what could have perhaps been a dirge-filled, melancholic event into a celebration, eliciting screams, yells, claps, and stomps from the emotional crowd, reveling, hooting, and hollering like an old-time preacher. The climax was a smoking audience-participation rendition of "This Land Is Your Land," followed by an equally rocking "Worldwide Rebel Songs." By this time, most in the crowd had left their seats (at Morello's urging) and gathered around the stage, shouting the lyrics and filling the room with emotion and energy.

The Skype connection, which was supposed to show Tomas on the movie screen above Morello throughout, didn't work for most of the set, but I could see Tomas and Claudia's faces on the screen of a laptop perched on a stool near the stage, heads bobbing to the music, giving the occasional thumbs-up. The setup worked as advertised for the final couple of songs, displaying Tomas on the movie screen above the stage, the massive image of his bearded face observing the night's events from on high like God almighty himself.

Morello wrapped up with an unplanned "Until the End," easing the tempo considerably yet escalating the emotional intensity of the evening. I looked up at the image of Tomas for a moment before returning my gaze to Morello—when I realized that he had missed a line. He had tears streaming down his face and was overcome with emotion, unable to sing.

A tired Tomas answered some questions from an equally tired crowd via Skype after the show, announcing to all his decision to stay alive for as long as he could bear his physical limitations. Cathy, seated among the crowd, stood and thanked everyone for their support, citing it as a significant factor in Tomas's decision to stick around.* Nights like these must, after all, help him understand that he can still very much have an impact despite the latest developments regarding his physical health.

When I was able to talk to Tom Morello a couple of weeks after the show, I told him I didn't know what to expect that evening.

---

* A chagrined Cathy later told me that Tomas hadn't given her any prior notification of his decision—she learned of it along with the rest of the theatergoers that night.

"Nor did I!" Morello responded. I told him I expected an extremely emotional event, but I didn't know which way it would go. It turned out to be a foot-stomping, cheering celebration of Tomas's life. "It's always my endeavor to rock the room, whether it's with a nylon-stringed guitar or whether it's with a bombastic band," Morello said. "And it was . . . it *is* a celebration of Tomas's *continuing* life, with the dramatic announcement that he's decided for now to continue to live, based in some measure on the global support and affirmation for his cause and sort of vindication of his worth in being alive that he received in the aftermath of his final letter—that was a great cause to celebrate."

I mentioned the tears I saw on Morello's face as he sang "Until the End." He said he had actually written the song, which contained the lines "I'll never turn, I'll never bend / I'm with you now until the end," "about more societal issues and my continuing in any circumstance to stand up for the underdog, but then, you know, songs take on shape and form a different context—and it's also a pledge of faithfulness to a friend, despite whatever circumstances might befall you."

I visit with Tomas the next morning. Jacob George, who performed at the tribute show the evening before, is there. He gives Tomas a copy of his CD, *Soldier's Heart*, and I buy a copy for myself. George's liner notes reveal that "soldier's heart" was a Civil War–era term for what is now known as PTSD. "My heart is wounded as a result of Moral Injuries and this album is an attempt to explore my wounds," he wrote.

Tomas tells me that he's already had several visitors this morning. "Three guys from the theater came here, and apparently I have an open invitation to a free movie whenever I want there," he says, clearly pleased by this gesture. The actor Charles Grodin, a friend of Phil Donahue, also stopped by for a visit this morning, followed shortly thereafter by Tom Morello, who gave Tomas last night's set list, which had been taped to the stage. It's now sitting on Tomas's bed, and I read the song names aloud. Tomas comments on a few of them. "'Stray Bullets,' one of the lyrics is about me,* and then that song he sang, 'Battle Hymns,' it's on the *Body of War* compilation. And apparently when I asked him to do it at the CD release party at South by Southwest in '07, he said that was the first time he had performed the song since he recorded it." He shares this information with pride, honored to have such stature among some of his favorite musicians and probably quite unaware that those musicians feel even more honored to know him.

After George leaves, Tomas remembers that it's been a while since he was last fed. "Claudia!"

"Yes, baby," she responds from the hallway.

"Do I need to be fed?"

It turns out that he does indeed need a feeding. "Do you want to see what that process is like?" he asks me. "Every three or so hours I have to be fed."

He can't really judge his feedings on whether he feels hungry, as he explains: "I'm still hungry after she feeds me." Other than keeping track of how long he's gone since last time, the only other indicator Tomas has that he needs to be fed is nausea, which comes occasionally if he goes too long without a feeding.

Claudia grabs a can of nutrient from the fridge in Tomas's bathroom. Tomas asks her to give it to me so I can read the label. "It's just the basic nutrients and proteins the body needs," he says. "I get 250 milligrams every three, three and a half hours. There's a tube here in my stomach," he says, lifting his shirt.

This is the first time Tomas has bared his upper torso to me, the first opportunity I've had to see his wounded body up close. He patiently and matter-of-factly points out each tube and scar, explaining its meaning.

---

* "Back of an Ace uncovered truck / The captain laughed and said 'Good luck' / As we rolled on through our first Iraqi town / From the rooftop we got blasted / Danny Lord's spine came unfastened / Stray bullets rainin' on down."

The front of Tomas's chest and abdomen is a maze of tubing. He has a permanent IV port in his upper right chest, for blood draws (Claudia says he is "a very bad stick") and this is also where the Dilaudid enters his body, supplied from the pain pump. There are the two bagged openings related to the removal of his colon—the distal and proximal stomas. A fourth tube, his feeding tube, is connected directly to his stomach. Yet another tube is the Foley catheter, which drains the urine from his bladder.

"I was shot right here," says Tomas, pointing to a small scar just below his left collarbone. "That paralyzed me. Luckily," he adds, applying a warped sense of logic, "it was the first shot that caused me to feel nothing, because the second shot was in my knee, and had I been shot there first, I would have been in a hell of a lot of pain. So I guess if there is a semblance of a silver lining to this story, it's that I got shot here first so I couldn't feel the pain of getting shot in the knee."

I ask Tomas how the bullet managed to get through his flak vest—was there a seam, or did it travel through an uncovered area like the arm hole? He smiles. "The flak vests we had had ceramic plates right here and right in the back," he says, pointing to his chest, "that would just crack on impact of say, an AK-47 round, but up here"—he points to his collarbone—"was just a layer of Kevlar and cloth, and so it went right through the shoulder pad of the bulletproof vest and then traveled in a downward trajectory and severed my spinal cord about the T4 level."

To the left of the entry point of his feeding tube is a dime-sized scar, which Tomas explains is where a previous feeding tube was inserted during his recovery from the initial injury more than nine years ago. A long scar that starts about four inches above his belly button and ends a few inches below it, circling his belly button, is still red from the much more recent removal of his colon.

Claudia attaches a large syringe, with plunger removed, to the feeding tube. She fills the syringe with nutrient and watches as it gravity-feeds into Tomas's stomach. Once the feeding is complete, she flushes the tube with water to prevent clogging.

Tomas asks Claudia for a cigarette. He also asks her to put the *Soldier's Heart* CD into his iTunes library. "Claudia thinks that when I ask for a cigarette it signifies the end of the conversation," Tomas explains, by way of apology, "but I said, 'No Claudia, if I could get a cigarette myself and light it then there would be no break in the conversation.'" While Claudia is putting the CD into her laptop, I grab a cigarette for Tomas, put it between his lips, and light it as he inhales.

When Claudia is finished importing the CD, she picks up a pack of Batman comic-book cards Tomas recently bought on eBay. She spreads them out on the bed and picks them up individually, showing them to Tomas and me. As we're looking at them, Garett comes in to say goodbye. I leave them alone.

After Garett leaves, Claudia opens the door next to Tomas's bed, which leads to the backyard and beyond, over the fence and down the hill to an open expanse of grass leading to a nearby school. The sunlight streams in. The doorway to a beautiful, sunny day beckons just inches from where Tomas lies in his hospital bed. The fresh, bright air mingles with the darkness and smoke in Tomas's room.

I ask Tomas about the *Where the Wild Things Are* tattoo that covers his right forearm. He says he got it back around 2007. "I liked the book as a child, and figured I'm not really into scary tattoos like skulls and shit, so I got this. So little kids look at me and go, 'Oh wow—*Where the Wild Things Are*!' And twenty-seven-year-olds can go, 'Oh wow—*Where the Wild Things Are*!—I read that as a kid!' And fifty-year-old kindergarten teachers are telling me about how they used to read it to their classes all the time." Clearly, it's become tiresome. "When I first got it, I welcomed the small talk about it, but once I got really sick and was in pain all the time, whenever I'd go to the ER at the VA, all I wanted to do was get in a bed, get some painkillers and try to rest, but the nurse is like, 'Oh—*Where the Wild Things Are*! Oh wow!' And a couple of times I've had to say, 'Please—I'm not trying to be rude, but could you just . . . I don't need the small talk.'" His voice tapers off at the end of this statement. He exhales and wears a weary expression.

Tomas is planning on attending a *Monday Night Raw* wrestling event downtown this evening. This cuts our time together short, as he wants to take a nap before heading out. I shake his hand, say goodbye, and leave the room with Claudia. I talk to her in the kitchen for a while before departing. I tell her that it's encouraging to see that he's at least trying to get out, and ask if he does this much. "No," she responds. "We have got a lot of good tickets and planned things that he hasn't gone to. We were trying to get him out to see *42*, the Jackie Robinson film. I got him in the chair, and he was in the chair for like five minutes, and he was like—he just couldn't do it, he's so tired to be in the chair."

She says she can pretty much tell when Tomas isn't going to be well enough to go out, but "instead of me saying 'you're not going to be well enough'—I can't do that. I don't want to be the buzzkill, 'cause what if he is well enough to go? I suspect that if we do go, we'll leave early, but at least he gets to see a bit, you know we did go to WrestleMania [a couple of years ago in Atlanta], so it's just . . . every day is different."

Tomas had called his old friend Roy McHugh about a month ago about going to Monday Night Raw. The pair had watched wrestling on TV together back when they were kids, and recently McHugh came over to watch wrestling specials in an attempt to spend more time with his friend. "I hadn't been watching it really, you know?" he said. "That was like one of his things, like he always gets those pay-per-views now—it's seventy bucks! So I would go over there and watch that with him, and I would try to watch it some here and try to get back into it. He called me up, and this was after he told me he was going to kill himself—or die, or whatever you want to call it—sometime after April, when his wife and him had their anniversary, and he's asking me if I want to go see wrestling with him at the end of May. So I just said yes, 'cause that means you're still going to be here and not die!"

Cathy, Nathan, and Tomas (right), 1983 (Cathy Smith)

Nathan, Lisa, and Tomas, 1997 (Cathy Smith)

Tomas (second line from left, nearest to camera) marching in formation during first boot camp, Fort Leonard Wood, MO, 1997 (Cathy Smith)

Cathy and Tomas after basic training during his first enlistment, Fort Leonard Wood, 1997 (Cathy Smith)

Timmy and Tomas, 2002 (Cathy Smith)

Riley Soden manning the gun on a Humvee on the morning of Black Sunday, Sadr City, Iraq, April 4, 2004 (Riley Soden)

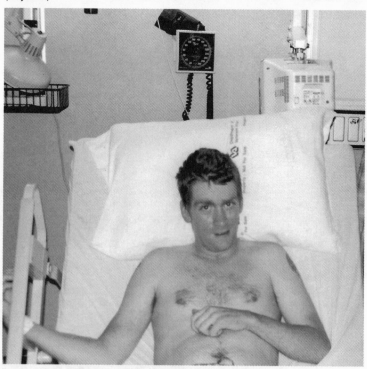

Tomas at Jefferson Barracks, Saint Louis, May/June 2004 (Cathy Smith)

Cathy and Tomas outside Jefferson Barracks, MO, 2004 (Cathy Smith)

Tomas and Riley Soden, Kansas City, 2005 (Riley Soden)

Tomas, Cathy, and Brie at a rally in Washington, D.C., August 2005 (Cathy Smith)

Tomas and others in the Washington, D.C., office of California Representative Henry Waxman, 2005 (Cathy Smith)

Nathan and Tomas the day before Nathan's first deployment to Iraq, Nashville, November 2005 (Cathy Smith)

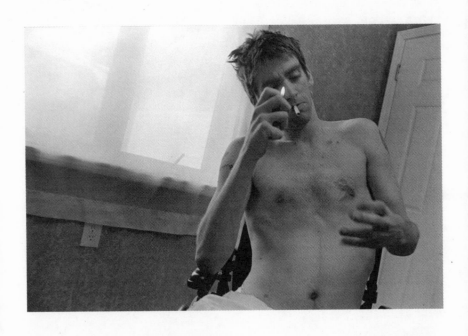

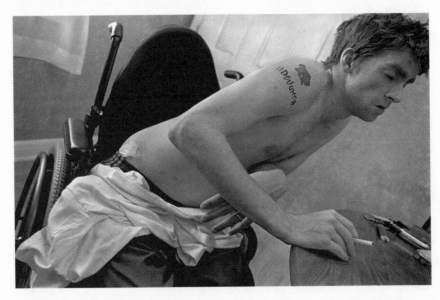

Tomas at home, Kansas City, February 2006 (Eugene Richards)

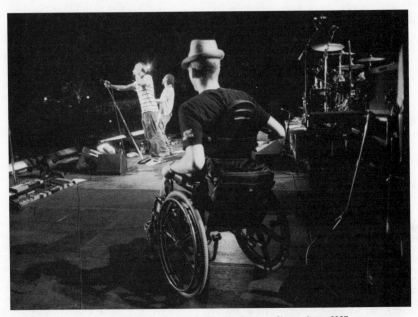

Above: Tomas watching Eddie Vedder and Ben Harper onstage, Lollapalooza, Chicago, August 2007
(Danny Clinch)

Opposite: Tomas and Eddie Vedder, Chicago, 2007 (Danny Clinch)

Tomas, New York City, 2008 (Danny Clinch)

Tomas at a screening of *Body of War*, Nashville, May 2008 (Alan Messer)

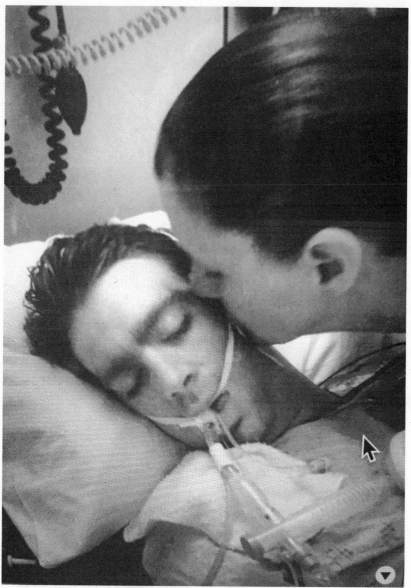

Cathy kissing her son, in a coma after the embolism, Saint Luke's Hospital, Kansas City, late May/early June 2008 (Phil Donahue)

Tomas, Chicago, November 2008 (Olivier Morel)

Tomas and Claudia, Chicago, November 2008 (Olivier Morel)

© PHOTOGRAPH BY ALAN MESSER ALANMESSER.COM

Tomas at home in Kansas City, showing off his *Where The Wild Things Are* tattoo, December 2009 (Alan Messer)

Timmy, Tomas,
and Phil Donahue,
Kansas City, 2011 or 2012
(Claudia Cuellar)

A line of Patriot Guard Riders salute Tomas as he makes his way toward a memorial service for his mother's stepfather Dale Wallen, a Vietnam-veteran Navy SEAL who died of Agent Orange–related illnesses, Osceola, MO, September 2011. (Cathy Smith)

Tomas and Claudia on their wedding day, April 20, 2012 (Claudia Cuellar)

Tomas, Claudia, and Peaches at home in Kansas City, 2013 (Eugene Richards)

Tomas and Claudia at home, Kansas City, 2013 (Eugene Richards)

Tomas at home in early 2013. "Claudia gave me this photo during my first visit. It was pinned to the back of my desk throughout the writing of this book." —MW (Claudia Cuellar)

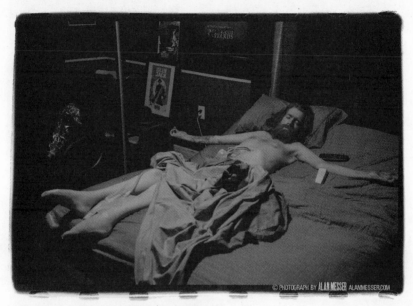

The body of war. Tomas at home, August 2013 (Alan Messer)

Tomas, Claudia, and the paw of Peaches, Kansas City, 2013 (Alan Messer)

Tomas in Portland, 2014 (Claudia Cuellar)

The last photo taken of Tomas, Denny Park, Seattle, November 3, 2014 (Claudia Cuellar)

Cathy's *Where The Wild Things Are*–themed tribute to her son, on her left wrist (Cathy Smith)

Chapter 9

Living Solo

We send countless irreplaceable human beings to this war, human beings who will never see a child graduate, never go to a family wedding—and we stand there and allow it to happen, again and again and again. We make movies that glorify war and ignore the real pain of war. And we blow the door wide open for any president to go to war whenever he wants to. And every president seems to think going to war is the only way he can show he has balls. We wage war after war—and nobody seems to be embarrassed by this. Well, it's time to tell the stories that do more than glorify sacrifice. It's time to tell the stories that make us want to put an end to war, once and for all.

—Phil Donahue

By fall 2006, things were quieter at Tomas Young's Kansas City home than they had been since he'd moved in back in late 2004. The yearlong filming of *Body of War* was now complete and Brie was gone. For the first time, Tomas was living alone. Despite some initial doubts, he had learned to care for himself and was enjoying this new sense of independence. "One of the big hurdles that kept me from asking for the separation sooner was because I was worried that I wouldn't be able to function as well on my own," Tomas remarked at the time. "I'm actually getting food for myself," he said, sitting in the kitchen near his refrigerator and microwave. "I'm not cooking yet—I'm still a nuclear chef."

Tomas had undergone surgery recently to remove more bullet fragments from his left knee after a blood test detected elevated lead levels. He asked a nurse if he could keep the bullet fragments. "They said, 'Yeah, come back tomorrow, we need to sterilize it,' and they had thrown it away," he said, disappointed. He had wanted to display it on a shelf as a conversation starter: "Somebody just comes to your house," he began playfully—"'What's that?' 'Oh—that's shrapnel that was taken out of my knee!'"

Tomas's focus on activism continued. His involvement with IVAW deepened for a time after the completion of the film. In August 2006, he and Riley Soden attended the fledgling organization's first national meeting, held at a Veterans for Peace convention in Seattle. "I remember it was at the University of Washington," Tomas recalled. "Everybody had gone home for summer break or whatever, and so they put me and [Soden] in this room and it was not suitable for my needs, so we had to go over to where the football players lived, and you could tell right away that the football players get treated pretty well, 'cause not only did they get this big-ass room with a king-size bed and everything, but downstairs there was this play area with a giant TV and a ping-pong table, and I was like, man, I need to play sports!" It wasn't just the dorm room that didn't meet his needs as a paraplegic. Soden recalls that a "good portion" of the convention area wasn't wheelchair-accessible either, "but we made it work."

Riley and Tomas didn't know what to expect from the gathering, which included several veterans' rights and antiwar organizations. "It was the first thing that we had done with IVAW," said Soden. "I liked their cause, but I was a little disconcerted when we got there to the meeting when I realized that Tomas and I were the only two that had been wounded who were in the organization at the time. So that kind of . . . I mean, you know, I appreciate what they were doing, but it just didn't feel right to me at the time. So I kind of backed off my involvement a little bit."

Tomas was nominated for the IVAW's board, a position he reluctantly accepted. "I didn't nominate myself, 'cause I didn't want to be on this board," he explained, "but I went up and gave this speech saying that I think what we need to do is counter-recruit. Take the guys and girls who ever served, get them into high schools and have them tell students the real story about joining the military. And I think that was what got me voted in. I didn't vote for myself—not because I didn't think I was qualified for the job; I just thought there were nine people more qualified than me."

The following month, Tomas attended the group's first board meeting in Philadelphia. He quickly became disillusioned. "Everybody was raising hands, trying to get everybody on board to do their own project, each one having their own ideas," he said. "It felt to me like there were too many chiefs and not enough Indians." After about three months, Young tendered his resignation from the board, citing a lack of organizational focus, particularly regarding care for returning veterans. He remained sympathetic to the organization's cause and would continue to advocate for IVAW, just not in a leadership role.

Meanwhile, Nathan Young was nearing the end of his twelve-month rotation in Iraq, based in Taji, about twenty miles from Sadr City, north of Baghdad. Although he was an artilleryman by trade, Tomas's younger brother spent the entire year working more in the role of infantryman, providing convoy security on treks all across the country.

It was a stressful, chaotic deployment. Nathan recalled one particularly harrowing moment when his convoy rolled out of the gate and immediately struck an IED. He watched in horror as the convoy's lead vehicle—normally the position his truck occupied—was rocked by an explosion and quickly became engulfed in flames, exacerbated by a five-gallon can of diesel fuel in the truck's bed. "We thought the crew was still inside the truck; we thought they were done," he said.

Somehow, the crew escaped the fire and survived. Memories of the explosion and other similarly chaotic events wore heavily on Nathan. When it was time to come home, he chose to decompress at his brother's house. Tomas had plenty of room and enjoyed the company. "I went on thirty days' leave and actually I spent pretty much the whole thirty days at his house," Nathan said. He was impressed with how his brother was faring—"I thought he was doing pretty good; he was getting around on his own," he recalled. Tomas had moved his bed out to the living room and the pair hung out there together, talking and playing video games. "About the whole thirty days I did that," Nathan said.

In late 2006, not long after Nathan had returned to Fort Campbell, Tomas once again found himself with a roommate. Riley Soden had been a regular visitor since being discharged from the Army in early 2005 and was looking for somewhere to live in north Kansas City. Tomas had a spare room and enjoyed the company of his good friend. "We wanted to hang out more together," said Soden, "and he kind of needed me to help him with some things. A lot of things he took care of himself, but with a little extra help and somebody that had been through the military with him, I just think it was a good fit."

Soden wanted to help his friend remain engaged in as active and full a life as possible. Admitting that "it definitely was a difficult moment when I first saw him" after the injury, Soden said that "pretty quickly I kind of realized that this is reality, and this is what we're going to deal with, and so I've done my best over the years to try to make him feel as adjusted to how he used to be, you know, when he could walk, as I could. . . . I kind of said, we're still going to live our lives and do the best we can with what we've got. And when Tomas and I lived together and hung out together a lot, we did a lot of traveling and seeing music and trying to go out. I didn't want him being inside, stuck in one spot."

The pair traveled to destinations both near and far. They visited local bars and music venues in Kansas City—they saw a Dave Matthews Band concert there—and flew to Austin, Texas, to visit Ellen Spiro, taking in a Michael Franti gig at Stubb's during the trip. They drove to Fort Campbell, Kentucky, to visit Nathan, and attended a hockey game in nearby Nashville, Tennessee, while they were there.

Getting out and about was often taxing, both physically and mentally. "It takes a lot of energy and effort to get around and just get into places and get to the right seating, and so Tomas got tired real quickly a lot, so there were times when he'd just want to leave," said Soden. "I always kind of felt that there was a little bit of anxiety or uncomfortableness that Tomas had in some situations where he would just kind of say, 'I'm not feeling this and I just really want to get out of here.' So there were times when we would have to leave things prematurely but there were times that we didn't want to leave. . . . There were times when the handicap accessibility of the places we went to wasn't that good, and I would pretty much—I'm a big guy so I would pull him places and deal with it. I would make it work for us, you know—I didn't want the fact that we couldn't go up a certain stairway or something stop him from having a good time."

The pair traveled to Chicago in August 2007 for the Lollapalooza music festival, where they spent the weekend appearing on behalf of IVAW and met with activist-artists such as Ben Harper and Eddie Vedder. Wheelchair access in a festival environment is typically less than ideal, something which was not lost on Vedder, who saw Tomas several times that weekend in between performing with Harper on the festival's opening night and in his customary role with Pearl Jam two nights later. "My main concern throughout all that was Tomas's well-being," Vedder recalled. "Festivals can be a bit of a clusterfuck, and they have a tendency to be muddy, and the stage can be a quarter-mile, a golf cart ride away from where the little trailers are for the dressing rooms. I wanted to make sure that there was wheelchair access and that there were ramps—I was just really trying to make sure that Tomas was comfortable."

Tomas sat at the side of the stage during Pearl Jam's set. In between songs, Vedder checked on Tomas, who wore his vest with cooling packs to combat the hot, humid weather. "I was just glad that he pulled it off," said Vedder. "They had to take him off the stage for a little bit and get him hydrated. So I was thinking about him this whole show, nervous for him. But he came out like a champ, and I got to introduce him to the crowd, and he introduced us and the song. It ended up being very powerful."

The song Vedder referred to was "No More," which he had written for *Body of War*.

During a chance meeting in early 2007, Phil Donahue had asked Vedder to compose a song for the film. Vedder immediately agreed. Soon ensconced in a Seattle studio, Vedder called an unsuspecting Tomas Young, who was so shocked to hear from one of his heroes that he almost dropped the phone. "Because it was a song that was going to be used for the film that was representing him, I wanted to make sure that he knew exactly what the lyrics were," said Vedder, "and I wanted to run everything by him and make sure it was—you know—spot on, because you were telling his story, so I wanted to make sure he had veto power."

The two men talked for an hour. "He asked if there was anything I wanted to be mentioned in the song, and I said, 'Well, we have this saying at the VA that nothing's too good for a veteran, and so nothing's what they'll get,'" said Tomas. "And so he put that in the song. And I told him about my atheistic beliefs and that's where he came up with the 'no more eulogizing.'"

The turnaround was immediate. Vedder set straight to work after hanging up. "I did it all in a day," he said. "I think I wrote *two* in a day . . . right after that conversation with Tomas, I think I stayed late that night."

Within days, Young and Donahue received an MP3 file via email of a new Eddie Vedder song entitled "No More," followed shortly thereafter by a second song, "Long Nights." The former served as a perfect, custom-built protest song, while the latter effectively portrayed Tomas's darker, more reflective periods. Tomas was floored at the notion of one of his musical heroes writing a song about him; Donahue was similarly impressed. "I got the signature song for our film, and I got Eddie Vedder's name on the poster," he said. "I was thrilled, 'cause it's a great demographic to bring in."

NO MORE

I speak for a man who gave for this land
Took a bullet in the back for his pay
Spilled his blood in the dirt and the dust
Now he's back to say:

What he has seen is hard to believe
And it does no good to just pray
He asks of us to stand
And we must end this war today

With his mind he's saying No More
With his heart he's saying No More
With his life he's saying No More war

With his eyes he's saying No More
With his body he's saying No More
With his voice he's saying No More war

Nothing's too good for a veteran
This is what they say
So nothing is what they'll get
In this new American way

The lies we were told to get us to go
Were criminal—let us be straight
Let's get to the point where our voices get heard
Behind the White House gates

With our minds we're saying No More
With our hearts we're saying No More
With our lives we're saying No More war

With our eyes we're saying No More
With our bodies we're saying No More
With our voices we're saying No More war

No more innocents dying
No more terrorizing
No more eulogizing
No more evangelizing
No more presidents lying

With our minds we're saying No More
With our hearts we're saying No More
With our lives we're saying No More war

Lollapalooza marked the first public performance of "No More,"
sung by Vedder and guest Ben Harper near the end of Pearl Jam's
set late in the evening, when temperatures had mercifully cooled a
little. After the show, Tomas and some IVAW friends went back to
Vedder's hotel for a little post-performance celebration. "I remem-

ber he had smuggled a huge Folgers coffee can of pot somehow on the plane, and he did it in some kind of ingenious way," recalled Vedder with a laugh. "I was impressed and fearful at the same time. I was like, 'Well, let's smoke it all now so you don't have to bring it all back!'"

It was a period of relatively good health for Tomas, who knew that further complications were a real danger given the nature of his injury. The roommates were intent on living every day to the fullest. "[His health] has progressively gotten worse, you know," Soden said in 2013. "It's what we kind of expected, and so that's why we did what we did, 'cause I didn't know how long Tomas had to be him, and so I pretty much spent my time trying to take advantage of the health that he did have."

It was an unspoken understanding between the two friends. "Tomas is a smart guy and he assumes the same thing about me, and so we kind of, based on what we had seen, we knew what was going to happen, and it's just one of those things that you don't really talk about, you know, you just kind of . . . deal with it," said Soden, who described his approach as, "When it happens, it happens, but until that day happens, I'm going to do the best I can with what we've got. I was always trying to be encouraging and engaging, friendly, and all that with him."

A month after Lollapalooza, Tomas traveled with family and friends, including Riley Soden, to the Toronto Film Festival for the premiere of *Body of War*. Co-directors Phil Donahue and Ellen Spiro were on hand, as was Eddie Vedder. On a rainy September 11, 2007, *Body of War* premiered in Toronto's Isabel Bader Theatre, drawing prolonged and enthusiastic applause. It was the first time Tomas and Cathy had seen the completed movie, having only viewed a rough cut up to this point. "I remember first thinking that it was not like any documentary that I had ever seen. There were no talking heads, not a lot of dry facts. . . . It was a love story between a mom and her two sons," Cathy recalled. "I remember the standing ovation making me feel so proud that my chest wanted to explode—proud not only of my amazing son and what an inspiration he was, but also being able to be a part of something that would change people's lives." After the film's conclusion, Tomas rolled down to the front of the theater. "They gave me another standing ovation, and I answered some questions," he said. "And what I found out was a Q&A must mean, in Canada, stand up and make your own statement, forget about the guy at the front who's answering questions and just do your own little soapbox thing. So I finally get to a point and say, 'It's a Q&A for me—if you have your own opinions, write a letter to the editor, do whatever you want, but this is questions-for-me time.'" He would later discover that this phenomenon was not particular to just Canada.

Cathy remembered turning to Phil Donahue's wife, Marlo Thomas, after the premiere to say, "What a shock it is to see your ass on the big screen for the first time," she recalled, adding, "Tomas chimed in and said, 'Yup, but did you see the size of my penis?'"

The high point of the night for Tomas was when Vedder came up on stage beside him and performed "No More." "I just remember thinking, 'Wow, I'm on a stage with Eddie Vedder while he's performing,' which I had to say a couple of times to make that sink in," Tomas recalled. "'I'm onstage with Eddie Vedder'—if you had told me this when I was thirteen, I would have said, 'That wouldn't happen—I'm not going to know Eddie Vedder.'" After thinking about this for a few seconds, he then added, "And if you'd told me that right after I had gotten out of the Army that I was going to join up within five years and get shot and paralyzed in Iraq, I would've said, 'Huh? I'm not going back in.'"

Body of War benefited from a similarly warm reception at many other film festivals that fall. It was named an official selection at five of them, winning two audience awards for best documentary and securing the prestigious National Board of Review's Best Documentary of

2007 award. It also made the short list for the 2008 Academy Awards, coming tantalizingly close, but was not named as one of the five official nominees.* Young told the press at the time that he was "ecstatic— to a point" at the film's reception. "I'm happy that it's getting all this coverage, but only if it works. If five million people see this film but none of them are moved to action . . . I'll still consider it a flop. But if only five or ten people see it but if a majority of them do something to enact a change in their community—be it to stop the war or help veterans' issues—then I'll consider the movie a giant success."

Phil Donahue, too, was buoyed by the film's reception and was bracing for success. "I had visions of grandeur," he said. "I had thought I was going to be able to dump a lot of money on top of Tomas. I assured him from the beginning that I would take no profit from this film. Not a dime. And, you know, you walk around and start talking to yourself and you begin to think, maybe we have a real little gem here of a movie, and it will become a curiosity and all over America people will go to see this."

When *Body of War* began its rollout to the public in early 2008, the film's uncomfortable subject matter became an issue. Donahue put together a plan for a press blitz to coincide with the film's nationwide release, but he experienced great difficulty in getting the attention of the national media. "It was hard for us, for example, to get on daytime talk shows, because a wheelchair is a turnoff," Donahue recalled. "If you're watching daytime talk shows, it's a lot of laughs and kibitzing. They do some wonderful stuff along the way, but for the most part, they want to make people laugh."

"Disability is ratings death," Donahue added. "The wounded stories you see on CNN almost always feature veterans who've lost

---

* "The short list is made up of fifteen titles from which the five nominees are chosen," Phil Donahue explained. "We weren't in any theaters—we aired on Sundance channel, I don't know how many people saw that—and we didn't . . . you know, all these ads 'for your consideration' . . . we didn't have any of those. And so we were not chosen as one of the five. I will go to my grave wondering whether we were six or seven."

limbs and now have prostheses—who now run in marathons. That's a story of hope and resurrection, a story of coming out of the ashes of a terrible injury. The subject of our documentary would *love* to have a prosthesis. He's *jealous* of the guys with prostheses." An April 1 appearance by Donahue and Young on the *Today Show* was a rare example of national TV interest in the story.

The US premiere of *Body of War* took place on March 7, 2008, at Tivoli Cinemas in Kansas City, just days before the fifth anniversary of the beginning of the war in Iraq. Nearly four years had passed since Tomas had been injured. Other screenings took place in major cities nationwide over the coming weeks. "Landmark Theaters agreed to roll us out, which I learned in movie lingo means, 'We'll show you in major cities and see how you do,'" Donahue said. "So Ellen and I would do Q&As after the movie. We did New York, Boston, Chicago, L.A., and on the opening night the place would be jammed. I mean, I thought I was Fellini. And the next night, there were six people in the theater."

The bubble had burst. "We sold no popcorn," Donahue said. With little money left for promotion and a subject matter that many found unpalatable, *Body of War* stalled. Despite Donahue's best efforts to promote the film, attendance was poor. "Theatrical marketing is democratic, it's honest," he said. "If you don't put people in the seats, it's hard to criticize a theater owner for not showing the movie. When you don't do that, the movie comes down immediately. There's a lot of expense, a lot of space, a lot of air conditioning, a lot of popcorn being unsold. . . . So we did not survive on the commercial circuit. No distributor would take our film. We did our best and we couldn't. . . . Nobody knew we were in theaters."

"We thought we had a hit single," Vedder added, "that this message and this film were going to cut through, even though it wasn't the usual glamorization of war, it was quite the opposite, and it really felt like it was a rocket, ready to take off. And it kind of did—there was lift-off, you know? And all the reviews were good, and the press was good, the interviews were great . . . but it was just hard to get people in the theaters to see a documentary about a wounded vet."

Eddie Vedder and Tomas Young continued to talk frequently by phone after the songs for *Body of War* had been written and record-ed, enough that by the time the two first met—at the studio in Se-attle to hear the recently completed songs—Vedder felt they already knew each other well. "I felt like we were already pretty close," he said, "because there were at least a half-dozen phone calls up to that point, just checking in on him and seeing how he was doing. Those conversations made me able to connect with the whole situation of war and a war of choice, and the hard-core realities of what happens to people when they return home, having issues finding care."

"As someone who's always been pro-diplomacy," Vedder said, "you sometimes get accused of being anti-soldier, you know—an-tiwar means anti-soldier—and nothing could be further from the truth, because you're wanting to protect those very same lives and support them, and make sure that they're not put in harm's way for, let's say, corporate interests and being caught up in the disposable human element of the military-industrial complex. So for me, it was a personal connection with the issue, and I was able to get an edu-cation. At the same time, I got to know an incredible person, and I think the conversations made him feel good, too—he was finding it to be a bright spot. They were pretty inspiring conversations, so yeah—I was trying to keep in touch as much as I could."

The pair naturally talked about what they had in common, which turned out to be a great deal. Music was an obvious starting point. "We would have three-hour conversations about music, ev-erything from Public Enemy and Whodini to Disposable Heroes and Michael Franti," said Vedder, who recalled that politics and philosophy were other topics of discussion, from "Cornel West and

Ralph Nader and . . . you know. He was really well educated and his opinions were all well founded." This, despite the fact that it was usually in the middle of the night when they talked. "It would be one o'clock my time and three o'clock his, and we were still going strong, and we would just laugh hysterically, and . . . I remember I would take notes of those conversations about, you know—things to write about, or things to be able to talk about in future days."

A friendship quickly developed, based more on the phone calls than any personal meetings. "When we'd see each other there would always be a bit of a crowd around and it was always a little tricky, and then it would be like, all right, grab a couple of photos to document the night and then take a few photos with this friend and that friend," Vedder recalled, "but then it was like, 'I'll call you after the show,' or 'I'll call you tomorrow.' Then I got a day off, and we'd talk for three hours again."

Back in August, while in Chicago for Lollapalooza, Vedder had offered to purchase Tomas a better wheelchair. "It was such a big concern around that weekend in Chicago, knowing that he was going to be doing press and knowing that he was going to have to be moving around and navigating through these situations and theaters and speaking engagements and interviews and TV stations," Vedder said. "I just wanted him to have a wheelchair that *worked*. And I told him that I'd talked to the band about it, that it wasn't just me, but that we were going to take it on as a group and we were all going to pitch in, and it was important and . . . please accept this gift."

Tomas politely thanked Vedder, and said he'd like to take some time to think about it. Vedder told me that he expected Tomas to eventually accept, but Tomas respectfully declined. "That was the way I felt, because I don't respect people who quote/unquote 'sell out' or take advantage of their situation," Tomas recalled. "I mean there are a lot of handicapped veterans who don't know Eddie Vedder or Tom Morello or Phil Donahue. . . . If I were in the shoes of a normal paralyzed veteran who didn't have everything that I had, and if I had seen me in a fancy, super-duper wheelchair that got bought by my rock 'n' roll friends, I'd think, 'That guy is a sellout,' and not truly understanding of what I went through."

"He came back and said, 'When I go out and speak, and people see me, I want them to see what we get,'" Vedder recalled. "He said, 'I want them to see that this is the janky wheelchair that'—you know, the brakes were always failing on it, it was just this *janky* wheelchair—'I want them to see how we're taken care of. That's part of what I'm representing.'

"I totally respect his decision and understand it, and it wasn't a surprise. I related to him. We had many things in common as far as not being in it for—he wasn't necessarily comfortable with the attention. He wanted the attention to be on the cause, and so he was taking on a schedule that wouldn't have been tough for somebody *without* all these other challenges. We were just hoping we could help facilitate it being a little easier."

A few months later, Tomas's wheelchair flipped backward in his driveway in Kansas City. His head hit the concrete. "I was rolling up the ramp to get in my van," Tomas recalled, "and I was bent over so I could get the momentum to work up the ramp, and I had a severe abdominal spasm that knocked my body back, and that knocked the wheelchair back. So it was just a freak thing." Vedder told me that if Tomas had had a better wheelchair, it wouldn't have happened. Tomas disagreed when I asked him about it in 2013—"It wasn't anything to do with my wheelchair," he said, but later allowed, "But it wouldn't happen to me now, because the wheelchair I have now is well-padded and I can't bend over anymore." However, a better wheelchair—one equipped with rear anti-tip stops—would absolutely have prevented this accident.

Tomas was admitted to the hospital, where he was diagnosed with bleeding on the brain. Despite hitting his head hard, he said he didn't fracture his skull.

A couple of months later, the wheelchair he had requested from the VA more than six months earlier was ready to be picked up. When asked what color frame he'd like, he said, "I want dark blue, like the color on the map for a state that votes Democrat."

Vedder continued to offer help. "I was like, well, all right, I don't want to ask him for money," Tomas recalled. Instead, he asked if Vedder would help to curate an album of antiwar songs which would further Tomas's message and also help to promote the film.

Vedder got the ball rolling at the *Body of War* premiere at the Toronto Film Festival, getting commitments for the project from music-industry executives and longtime Pearl Jam associates Michele Anthony and Michael Goldstone. Then, as he recalls, he "put it all in Tomas's hands to curate it." Tomas began drawing up a list of songs for inclusion in the collection, often bouncing ideas off Vedder during their long late-night phone calls. "He had an epiphany that it should really be a wide range of music, and that was all him," said Vedder. "All I did was agree and laugh and listen, and then say, yeah, let's try it, let's see what we can do."

Once a song list had been drawn up, Vedder and Young wrote a letter to the artists requesting their permission to use the songs. "We were asking for their contributions and their support from a personal level," Vedder recalled. They figured on about a 50 percent success rate, so the song list was enough to fill two CDs, while the plan was for a single-CD release. The requests were far more successful than anticipated—the majority of the requests were granted, necessitating the collection's expansion to a two-CD set. The resulting collection was titled *Body of War: Songs that Inspired an Iraq War Veteran*.

It was an eclectic assortment of songs, reflecting Tomas's diverse musical interests and his perspectives on war and politics. "I love the fact that it has Tomas's fingerprints all over it," said Vedder. "It's like a mixtape on vinyl." The collection included Brendan James's "Hero's Song" alongside Lupe Fiasco's "American Terrorist," which was followed by songs from Michael Franti and Rage Against the Machine. Hip-hop artist Talib Kweli and academic/activist Cornel West contributed "Bushonomics," while other inclusions were from Public Enemy, Bruce Springsteen, System of a Down, Tom Waits, Roger Waters, Neil Young, and Pearl Jam. Eddie Vedder and Ben Harper's rendition of "No More" from the 2007 Lollapalooza festival was also included. Another inclusion, the Bouncing Souls song "Letter from Iraq," was based on a poem written by Tomas's friend Garett.

"These are songs I selected because they helped inspire and motivate me," Tomas said at the time. "I want this album to open people's eyes, to not only prompt them to move their feet but also move their minds. Ever since I was a teenager, I've found solace in music. Coincidentally, a lot of the music I listened to when I was a confused and misguided teen was by Pearl Jam. So my life has come full circle, for Eddie to have written a song about me and for him to appear on an album for which I served as executive producer."

Body of War: Songs that Inspired an Iraq War Veteran was released by Sire Records on March 18, 2008. The label donated $100,000 to IVAW in Tomas's name.

To mark the collection's release, and also to promote the film which had undergone its US premiere just a few days earlier, Tomas traveled to Austin, Texas, for the annual South by Southwest music festival, which took place in mid-March. Young attended a packed screening of the *Body of War* film on March 13, which was followed by a standing ovation and a Q&A with the audience. "I was never interested in public speaking," Tomas told the *Los Angeles Times* during his visit, "but people tell me I'm a natural. Maybe I should have developed an interest in it earlier. Maybe it would have kept me out of the military."

Later that night, Tomas was an onstage guest at Stubb's Bar-B-Q for a special event which celebrated the release of the collection of songs for *Body of War*. Several artists whose songs appeared on the collection—Tom Morello, Serj Tankian, Brendan James, Ben Harper, Rx Bandits, and Kimya Dawson—performed that evening.

Tom Morello had first become aware of Tomas's story when Tomas asked to use Morello's song "Battle Hymns" from his solo act, the Nightwatchman, and the Rage Against the Machine song "Guerilla Radio" for the collection. "I was happy to grant him the Nightwatchman song, and Rage was happy to grant the other song to the soundtrack," Morello recalled. "We crossed paths at South by Southwest . . . he was there promoting the film; I was there on tour. We did some joint press to promote *Body of War*."

When I asked Morello what made him empathize with Tomas's situation, he responded, "To me, it was less being empathetic, and more being inspired. After watching the film, I believe there's nothing more courageous than a soldier who's willing to stand up against an unjust and immoral war, and Tomas was that in spades, you know? Despite his physical condition, he was on this global press tour to try to stop this awful war, and putting all of his energy and considerable intellect and sense of humor and fortitude into spreading the gospel of peace."

About a month after South by Southwest, Tomas and Morello met again, this time in Washington, D.C. Morello, along with other artists, was in the midst of the Justice Tour, a two-week outing that combined activism and music with a focus on social justice. The Washington stop focused on peace and veterans' issues, featuring a show at a local nightclub and a visit to Walter Reed Army Medical Center. It was Tomas's first visit to the facility since his hospitalization back in 2004. "In each city we would do some act of social justice, and then play a show that would benefit that," Morello recalled. "So that particular show was to benefit IVAW, and Tomas was kind of our tour guide through Walter Reed, and we stopped and visited a number of soldiers' rooms. Some of them had been back only a couple of days from these horrendous injuries, and . . . you know, the lure is that some of these people are fans of rock, and I think it was myself and Boots Riley, and I'm not sure who else on that particular date . . . Wayne Kramer might have been there. . . . You know, maybe they wanted to meet some guys in bands, but then quickly, the focus of attention was on Tomas's conversation with them—someone who could speak, in the language of a soldier, about the injuries that they had, about how he was dealing with that, and also about the soldier and veteran antiwar movement."

"That was the first time I had been back there," Tomas recalled, "and I was there just basically to say, 'See, look at me, I was in this hospital just like you, two or three years ago,' and . . . maybe I gave them a false hope 'cause I was with these rock stars and things. I was like, 'It really does get better.'"

Tomas's ability to connect with these injured soldiers impressed Morello and took him aback somewhat. "There was this one kid who was literally *cut in half*, I mean he was sort of . . . nothing below the chest, and with a twenty-two-year-old wife," Morello said, recalling that he watched Tomas interact with the wounded soldier. "And it's like Tomas played a role as both a healer and inspirer in telling people, not only can you live, you can make a difference in your world."

Tomas said he didn't remember the person Morello was talking about, then offered a profound observation as to why. "I guess that's a habit of severely injured people, is they look past the injury and just focus on the person," he said. "The focus of the able-bodied person is to focus on the injury and not the person."

Spring 2008 saw Tomas Young back home, alone again, since Riley Soden had moved out after changing jobs. The *Body of War* film had failed to find a substantial audience, but through the film, its companion music compilation, and his appearances across the nation, Tomas had attracted a significant amount of attention. "If people want to meet me because I'm thrust in the limelight, hopefully I can turn that enthusiasm on its ear," Tomas told the *Los Angeles Times* while at South by Southwest. "To get them involved, whether on a small scale, like helping out at a homeless shelter or veterans' shelter, or a large scale, like actively protesting Congress."

"I want there to be a sharp decline in military enlistments," he told *Billboard*. "I don't want to see another American or Iraqi son or daughter in a situation like I am, or worse. I want veterans to receive the proper attention and care, because many of them don't have the means or the opportunity to go outside of the system to seek the health care they so desperately need."

He was an eloquent and effective speaker who was just beginning to hit his stride in those early months of 2008. In an interview with *Smith Magazine* that April, Tomas said, "You heard a lot of talk for a while about those of us in the antiwar movement emboldening the enemy with our antiwar statements, but what emboldens a country like Iraq more than seeing 160,000 troops descend on the country for reasons that end up being false?" he said. "What emboldens an enemy more than hearing a song by the likes of Toby Keith reach such great heights and status that says, 'We'll stick a boot in your ass because it's the American way'?"

He shared his anger at the lack of public outcry against a war that was killing and maiming so many of his colleagues. "In Vietnam we had a draft because we had a very unpopular war," he explained. "That draft angered people so they took to the streets—fifty thousand–plus American soldiers were drafted, saw what they saw, and decided not to fight." Today's war, he said, affected such a tiny portion of the public—less than half a percent of the US population serves in today's military, as opposed to 4 percent during the Vietnam War and 12 percent during World War II—that it engendered little real action from them. "What you have is an overwhelming majority of American citizens opposing the war, but that involves taking a phone call going, 'Oh yeah, I don't like the war,' and hanging up and that's the end of your day," Tomas said. "Or you see a bunch of yellow ribbon magnets that say 'Support Our Troops.'

That involves a $3.99 investment at a gas station, but hey, you did your part. Not enough people are feeling the sting and sacrifice to really want to get involved."

"It's hit or miss," Tomas continued when the subject shifted to VA health care. "The VA staff is amazing. They do the best with what they can. Unfortunately, what they can do and what they get is lacking because we have veterans from Vietnam, Korea, the first Gulf War, even some from World War II that are still around and still need care, plus an influx of other soldiers. We have almost 29,000 people that are seriously injured. That doesn't count the tens of thousands more . . . who need psychiatric care, who are mentally injured. And that's going to cost money. They're estimating due to veterans costs this war will roughly cost between three and four trillion dollars, and that money needs to come from somewhere. The government will be quick to point out there has been increased VA spending, but not enough. It's still criminally underfunded.'" Young added, "I'll admit, though, right now my care at the VA has gotten pretty good. I don't know if it's because people are able to watch a documentary about me and my recovery or what—I've been told by people in the VA that's not the case, but I have been lied to by the VA before."

When asked if he felt that there was a "veterans' candidate" in the upcoming 2008 election, Tomas responded, "Well, it's certainly not the current veteran candidate [John McCain]. I believe his voting record would show he's the poorest in voting for veterans' benefits. I can see where he wouldn't understand veterans' care because he's on the Senate health plan, not going through the VA like a lot of other Vietnam vets have to do. At this point I would have to say Barack Obama is my candidate. Again, we're going on election-year promises, but he has pushed for better veterans' care. He came through

---

* By 2013, estimates as to the US cost of the wars in Iraq and Afghanistan had climbed to between $4 and $6 trillion.

for those of us who were at Walter Reed and had to pay for our own meals and phone calls."

Tomas's role as a public figure, a spokesperson for this new generation of injured warriors, was to be tragically short-lived. The coming weeks were to necessitate a focus once again on his personal well-being.

Chapter 10

Claudia

It's like what the war couldn't do, the medical system did.

—Roy McHugh

Nathan Young was supposed to be processed out of the Army on September 17, 2007. Instead, he found himself boarding a plane back to Iraq that very same day. He'd been stop-lossed: subjected to an involuntary extension of his service, through a policy implemented after 9/11 and expanded in 2004 to maintain the troop levels required to fight the wars in Iraq and Afghanistan. He wouldn't become a civilian until 2009.

Nathan's second deployment to Iraq began place just ten months after his return home from the first. It was a fifteen-month rotation, the first six months of which he spent firing artillery rounds in Tikrit and Baiji, in northern Iraq—at times, a *lot* of rounds. "We actually shot 250 rounds of artillery between two guns in nine days," he recalled. At least this was the actual job he'd trained for when he signed up, one that entailed a few degrees less chaos and uncertainty than the convoy security he'd pulled throughout his last rotation.

After about six months, Nathan's unit moved south to Camp Anaconda in Balad, just north of Baghdad—the town to which

Tomas had been airlifted on Black Sunday. A couple of months after the move, during a regular phone call with his mom, Nathan received grim news: His older brother had been found unconscious and was in the hospital, in a coma. Nathan was granted two weeks' emergency leave and was on a flight home within days.

Back in late 2007, Tomas had gone to the VA hospital in Kansas City complaining of pain and swelling in his right forearm. He was initially diagnosed with carpal tunnel syndrome and sent home with hydrocodone. Eventually, "they did an ultrasound and found that I had a clot in one of my veins," he said. "They put me on blood thinners to get rid of the clot, and everything was fine." Tomas embarked on the *Body of War* press rollout over the next few months and experienced no further problems with his arm.

Six months later, the prescription for the blood thinner—Coumadin—ran out. Shortly thereafter, on May 29, 2008, Tomas suffered a pulmonary embolism while he was home alone. The clot in his arm had dislodged and migrated to his chest, blocking a main artery to the lung. His friend Kelly found him unconscious in bed the following morning. "The sheets and blankets were all covered in shit and piss 'cause I had evacuated . . . you know—that's what you do when you die," he said. "The blood clot was still there, and after they had taken me off the blood thinners, it just re-formed and went into to my lung, and my brain got cut off from oxygen for a period of quite a few hours." He was rushed to Saint Luke's Hospital. At some point he fell into a coma. "I don't know, in the night I had the embolism and the anoxic brain injury, but I just know I woke up about three, four days later in a hospital. After one of the craziest dreams I ever had in my life."

A doctor later explained to Tomas that "when the patient presents with [deep vein thrombosis], it's standard procedure to give them six months of blood thinner and then take them off. . . . They don't check to see if it's gone . . . they don't even call you in to tell you that they're taking it off. And when he told me this, I was like, 'What? If I had been on it the whole time, this would never have happened!' I was so angry."

In his deeply moving book *The Diving Bell and the Butterfly*, author Jean-Dominique Bauby, who suffered a massive stroke and fell into a coma, writes, "As a rule, I do not recall my dreams. At the approach of day their plots inevitably fade. So why did last December's dreams etch themselves into my memory with the precision of a laser beam? Perhaps that is how it is with coma. Since you never return to reality, your dreams don't have the luxury of evaporating. Instead they pile up, one upon another, to form a long ongoing pageant whose episodes recur with the insistence of a soap opera."

Tomas had a very similar experience during his coma. "I thought it was real because it went on for days," he recalled. "I would go to sleep and wake up, and something would fall over, like a cup of water or something, just like the day before—just like *Groundhog Day*." Even in 2013, five years later, Young could recall long episodes of the dreams he experienced during his coma in vivid detail. And because he enjoyed talking about these dreams—and not about his own painful reality—Young's playful and imaginative character took over when he described them to me, and his pain and physical difficulties appeared to melt away, if only briefly. "At the time," Tomas began, "I was watching *Charmed*, this show about three sisters that are witches, 'cause I thought they were attractive and I like to get high and watch"—he paused, searching for the right words—"*magic shit* in the mornings." He laughed. "And so in the coma—in my dream world—first they worked in a morgue." Tomas then went on to describe his dream, which included the three *Charmed* sisters, himself, and a rather incongruous cage fighter, all in great detail, including dialogue between the characters, sights, sounds—even smells.

The coma dream continued, switching scenes and characters. The setting became a restaurant and a house; the *Charmed* sisters and cage fighter gave way to his mother and stepfather. But Tomas was in the same condition: "In almost all of my coma dreams," he said, "I'm lying in a bed of some kind and still hooked up to my machinery, and I can't talk." And in none of his dreams—even in his nightly dreams during normal sleep—could he walk. "People say that in their dreams, they can walk, even though they're paralyzed," he said. "I've not had that dream experience yet."

This second dream that Tomas recalled was loaded with more overt symbolism. His mother and stepfather and their home were all present. The home was on stilts, proving difficult to access, "and so my mom had my stepdad building a ramp all the way up to the house," he recalled. He said that the house/restaurant contained "all these balloons and flowers from my hospital room," which suggests that Tomas faded in and out of consciousness during the dream, noticing the balloons and flowers in his actual hospital room. "And," he added, "there was a doorway between the past, where I was, and the present tense."

Tomas remembers his mother talking to a man who was walking back and forth through the doorway between past and present. "He goes, 'There's this doorway, and there's a kid and he's lying on a bed and there's all this get-well stuff,' and she goes, 'Is that where my son is? You'd better go over there and bring all this stuff back to me.' And so all this stuff started disappearing and going through this door with this guy, and the last thing that she tells him to get is me." But, Tomas recalled, his mother's increasingly impatient demands, peppered with a few insults, angered the man: "He goes, 'She can go to hell.' And I was stuck there."

"I thought it was real life. It seemed real to me," Tomas insisted when I remarked upon the clarity of his memories. "It's interesting," he said, "because I'd been placed in a medically induced coma on the way from Kuwait to Walter Reed, and I didn't have any of these memories. I was in a medically induced coma when I got hit by a car when I was ten, and didn't have these memories. Was in a *self*-induced coma—although I didn't do it *to* myself purposely, it was just no medicine was used to put me in the coma, I had just gotten in a coma on my own—and that was when the visions started happening. So," he said, concluding with eyebrows raised, in deadpan mode, "if you're going to go comatose, be sure to do it to yourself—don't let the doctor do it to you."

There were still more layers to the coma dreams. In one of them, then-senator Barack Obama, campaigning for president at the time, entered Tomas's hospital room, wanting to shake his hand and refusing to leave until he did. Tomas remembered apologizing because he was unable to lift his arm. "I was like, 'You don't understand, Mr. President—I can't move,'" he said.

When Ellen Spiro heard the news of the embolism, she immediately traveled to Kansas City to be with Cathy and the family. Ellen and Cathy spent several days and nights at Tomas's bedside, taking a walk down to nearby Mill Creek Park at one point to participate in a rally for him.

About four days after he had been found unresponsive, Tomas began to slowly regain consciousness as Ellen and Cathy looked on. They had been playing him music, and eventually he began smiling and blinking his eyes. "I've never witnessed anything like that in my whole life," Spiro remembered of the surreal scene. "It's like seeing somebody be born again," she said. "It was a very intense experience. He was coming out a little more, a little more." He tried to explain the coma dreams to his loved ones, but found that he couldn't speak. What little was intelligible, Spiro recalled, "was all just odd and dreamlike—he was part there and part somewhere else."

"There was no official 'waking up' from the coma," Tomas said. "I felt like what was going on was going on in real life, so I would wake up one morning and . . . and I tried to get people to stay, so it was just like I woke up and [said], '*This* happened and *this* happened,' and people were like, 'None of that happened.'"

"When he woke up, you couldn't hear anything when he talked—like his lips would move, but you couldn't hear anything," Roy McHugh remembered, "and he always talked a mile a minute, so it was hard to understand what he said. I was just trying to read his lips and you'd hear like a faint whisper, maybe. He would get really, really, really frustrated." The fact that Tomas had a tracheostomy tube inserted in his airway helped to explain his difficulty speaking, but it turned out that the problem was more complex than that. He was having difficulty forming and pronouncing words—not just getting the air out to make a sound.

Young was also having trouble recognizing people—a sign of short-term memory loss. Another alarming development was that Tomas appeared unable to use his hands. When his speech difficulties became apparent, the hospital staff provided a board on which he could write what he was trying to say, but he couldn't grasp a marker. The dream where he'd been unable to use his hands had been eerily prescient.

When Nathan Young arrived at Saint Luke's Hospital in Kansas City, fresh from combat in Iraq, Tomas was conscious but back in intensive care. He had been returned to the ICU when a nurse gave him his pills orally, in applesauce, despite the fact that he was NPO (nothing by mouth). He inhaled the applesauce into his lungs. "He had no swallow reflex—even once they took the tube out, he couldn't swallow," said Cathy. "So that was another time that I almost killed a nurse."

Once Tomas's condition had stabilized, after about a month, it was determined that he would need rehab to help him regain at least some of the dexterity and strength he'd lost in his arms and hands. Cathy said he had "no grasp at all." The VA wanted him to use its facility; the Young family pushed back, wanting to send him instead to the state-of-the-art Rehabilitation Institute of Chicago. When the VA balked ("The VA didn't want us to go there," said Cathy, presumably due to cost), Cathy called their bluff. No problem, she said—they would enlist the help of some of Tomas's famous friends and organize a benefit concert to pay his way. She recalled that the next day, the VA informed her that it had reconsidered. Tomas was quickly transferred by air ambulance to the Rehabilitation Institute of Chicago, where he did daily rehab.

Ellen Spiro, who visited Tomas in Chicago, was impressed with the Rehab Institute's facility and staff. "I remember him working with the physical therapists, and I remember what a great facility it was in Chicago and what good care he was getting, and that was such a stark contrast to the VA," she said. "They had physical therapists, tons of them, working with people all the time; they never just left him there unless it was rest time or time to eat. The whole place had a completely different feel to it than the VA did. It was a healing place."

Cathy visited Tomas on weekends, eventually moving to Chicago so she could be close to him. She'd spent a great deal of time away from home over the past four years, caring for her son in Washington, D.C., and Saint Louis and traveling with him during his public appearances, and now she was facing a long commitment to help him while he was in Chicago. Her marriage, already strained, didn't recover. "All I know is what happened," said Cathy when asked to gauge the impact of her son's injury on her personal life. "I don't know what kind of effect it had because that's what it was."

"Yeah, my marriage fell apart," she continued, "but was it because of the embolism, was it because I was flying all over for the movie, was it because I wanted Tomas to move in with us after he was injured and my ex said no, was it because he didn't want me going back and forth to Chicago every weekend? You know, here was my son that didn't know anyone, couldn't speak, couldn't use his hands, in a hospital all by himself and I was supposed to not go? . . . I know so many people who have lost sons, who have had sons or daughters that were injured, and it's hard to say how things were affecting us, because it's just our life—it's just, you know—how did your flat tire affect you? I don't know how it did, it just happened and we moved on. . . . Yeah, I mean, sure, it affected my life terribly. But I think it made all of us just amazingly strong in the things that we've been through since then, with sick babies, and sick children, you know? And then again I suffer fools badly, you know, people that whine about their little piddly-ass daily problems, you know—oh, my neck, or oh, my shoulder . . . oh, I've got a flat tire . . . It's stupid. Shut up."

The speech and physical therapies that Tomas received in Chicago proved beneficial. He recovered a great deal of movement in his arms, but his strength and fine motor skills, particularly in his hands, remained markedly degraded. He was able to speak again, but it required great effort and his speech was slurred, which was endlessly frustrating to the eloquent Tomas. When I pointed out that the therapy in Chicago appeared to have made a huge difference, he was unwilling to go that far. "Yeah—it made a difference," he allowed. Then, after pausing: "Think of the difference that it would have made if I had never gotten a pulmonary embolism, and I would still be just a sweet little paralyzed young man."

When Eddie Vedder got the call about Tomas's pulmonary embolism, he was overcome with emotion. "It upset me to the core," he said, adding that he called a close friend in order to vent. "I was fucking weeping with rage, and I just paced the sidewalk, and we were able to talk through it . . . just all the complexities and how it just doesn't get better." Vedder was distraught. "These are what you want your politicians, Congress—everybody—to be aware of and to be deeply connected to."

After about two months of rehab, Tomas was sufficiently stable to be able to venture out of the facility and accept Vedder's invitation to attend his solo performance at Chicago's Auditorium Theatre on August 21. Vedder introduced Tomas to the audience, and he remained onstage, looking on as Vedder performed "No More." It was Tomas's first trip away from the rehab facility.

The next day, the phone rang in Tomas's room at the Rehabilitation Institute of Chicago. It was Claudia Cuellar.

A Chicago resident, Cuellar had been exposed to the city's National Vietnam Veterans Art Museum (now the National Veterans Art Museum) through a Vietnam-veteran boyfriend who was also an artist. "I went to kind of discover this person through the art," she said, "but then I discovered like this whole world. . . . I learned about war and the consequences of war and the effects it had on human life. And then to meet these veterans at this museum and to further get, like, this downloaded storytelling through all the mediums of art, poetry, photography, sculpture, painting . . . and to feel those individual stories of suffering that come from war and how devastating it is to the human spirit and the human psyche, you know, that was kind of imparted to me. And it left such an impression."

Cuellar delved further into the legacy of Vietnam, watching films such as Oliver Stone's searing *Born on the Fourth of July*. Meanwhile, the onset of war in Iraq drove home the point that a whole new generation was about to experience the consequences of war. "I was used to seeing fifty-five- and sixty-year-old men in wheelchairs, and amputees, and PTSD, but it was hard to start seeing twenty-year-olds like that," Cuellar said. "So when the [*Body of War*] movie came out I was really interested because I was like, 'Wow, finally somebody stood up against the administration.' And I wanted to meet this person, 'cause I just felt like . . . despite the difficulty that he suffered, he still found himself able to give something back, and to try to tell the story. Just like Ron Kovic did, you know?" She tried to contact Tomas but was unable to reach him.

A couple of months after she'd watched *Body of War*, Cuellar read an online review of Eddie Vedder's solo performance in Chicago and discovered that Tomas was in town. "I read the review and they said he was at the Rehabilitation Institute, and I had actually volunteered there—I knew of the institute because I was a clinical massage therapist," Cuellar recalled. "It was considered the top rehabilitation hospital in the country. And I just called."

She expected to talk to the Tomas Young she had seen in the film only a few months earlier. However, the person who picked up the phone wasn't Tomas—it was Ellen Spiro, who was visiting at the time. "She answered the phone," said Cuellar, "and she communicated for him, which I found a little confusing, but I thought maybe she was kind of just protecting him, just kind of screening the call. . . . I didn't know that he'd had the embolism and his speech had changed."

Cuellar, through Spiro, made arrangements to visit the following day. "When I showed up the next day, I was kind of shocked by what I saw," she recalled. "He was alone in this big room, and he had grown a big beard, and he looked so . . . exhausted, like he had lived a hundred lifetimes. I think he was surprised that I actually showed up. I noticed when he started talking that his speech had changed and that his hands seemed to be weak, and that he was very different from the film. So I sat down with him—actually I reached out my hand to him, because I knew at the hospital, they weren't touching him in a . . . you know, most people in a hospital, it's in a clinical way, so I wanted to just . . . connect with him, I guess. I felt like it was okay, and he told me everything that happened, and they had to kick me out." She offered to bring Tomas books, music, movies—"whatever I could do to make it better for him."

Claudia brought Tomas a book from the museum. "I wanted to explain what they were doing and share my background," she said. "And I kind of imagined there'd be more people there, but it wasn't his hometown, you know, so it did feel like he was really alone. It's hard to be alone—in the hospital, especially. I'm like, I can get people to come, you know, my friends who are veterans."

Cuellar even arranged a visit from *Fight Club* author Chuck Palahniuk, a favorite of Tomas's. "He ended up spending three hours with me," Tomas recalled, "just talking about . . . nothing. And it meant a lot."

Claudia's regular visits meant a lot to Tomas too. As the pair met more and more frequently, their feelings for each other deepened beyond simply friendship. "We could talk about everything," Cuellar said.

"He introduced me to a lot of cool music and we were both looking forward to this election, you know—Obama was our Kennedy, he was supposed to change everything, it was going to be the world we wanted, and so it was a kind of very exciting, intoxicating time. And there was a point where I maybe started developing feelings and I didn't . . . I wasn't sure, and I was embarrassed about it, and I was afraid to say something, 'cause I said, what if . . . He's in a vulnerable position, you know, who am I to come in there and . . . I don't know, I was confused by it and I didn't know what to do, but I really loved coming to see him. And then he had the same feeling where he was developing feelings for me but he didn't know how to say it because he didn't want to scare me away. And then he played that Michael Franti song—music was the way we communicated, so we'd play music and we'd talk about it, and so—Michael Franti, this 'Love Me Unique' song, and it was very suggestive, and it had very sensual lyrics, and I blushed, and it became . . . you know, we could see that we liked each other."

Cuellar's visits became a daily occurrence, and when she had to travel for work, the pair would frequently converse by phone. "If you had asked me before meeting Tomas if I could be with someone in a wheelchair as someone who is a lifelong physically active sports person," said Cuellar, "I would feel that it wouldn't be fair to the relationship 'cause it would be two different worlds trying to come together, but once I met him it just really became a matter of, you know—what can I do to be with this person? Because I'd just never felt that way with anybody before."

Cuellar reached out to friends and brainstormed other methods of learning as much as possible about being in a relationship with a paraplegic. "I wanted information," she said. "I wanted to know about other women in relationships and I figured you'd have to be creative, and I was sure that our feelings could transcend our physical limitations, and especially when you really love somebody, it doesn't matter what the situation is. The only citation that came up on the Internet when I keyword searched 'falling in love with a para' was this *Coming Home* film," Cuellar said, referring to the 1978 film starring Jane Fonda, Bruce Dern, and Jon Voight. In it, Fonda plays the wife of an officer who is deployed to Vietnam. When volunteering at the VA hospital, she meets a paraplegic veteran (played by Voight) and the two fall in love. Both Voight and Fonda won Oscars for their performances. "The tenderness and the humanity that she kind of saw in him and what he exhibited to her that was so different," said Claudia, "that was kind of the way I felt with Tomas."

"With Tomas," she explained, "he let me into his life. . . . His heart was completely open. People look at me and say, 'Oh, you're with a person that's in a wheelchair,' and I say, well, he can't walk, but his heart is totally open. He's loved me in a way that I've never really been loved before—unconditional, totally accepting, nonjudgmental, noncritical. He's got my back, he's for me in every way, so it's a very liberating, beautiful kind of love. When someone can see you for who you really are, there's nothing . . . *sexier* than that. There's nothing more incredibly exhilarating than someone who you don't have to hide yourself in front of. And sometimes it's a terrifying space when you're not used to it, 'cause you're so used to like compartmentalizing your whole life."

As winter approached, the improvements Tomas had made during rehab in Chicago became incrementally smaller and it became clear that he wouldn't fully recover from the injuries sustained from the anoxic brain injury. He was also growing impatient with his progress and was itching to get home. "They were trying to get him back to where he was before, but I think it became apparent over time that he wasn't going to be going back to being like a manual chair paraplegic," Claudia recalled. "He was considered a partial quad and he would need twenty-four-hour care. Before, he lived independently, he clothed himself, transferred himself, bedded himself, did his own bowel regimen, and he had a personal assistant come twice a week maybe. He had a year where he was on his own. He had kind of rolled that boulder up the mountain, he had learned how to be a para, and he was independent and functioning and living alone and enjoying it, having his home life—and then . . ."

Tomas went home in November 2008. As with his previous return to Kansas City, he would face a completely new reality, requiring around-the-clock care and assistance with many of the routine daily tasks he had previously been able to handle himself. Claudia was concerned about Tomas transitioning to twenty-four-hour care at home with new caregivers. "So I was like, I'll come help you, let's see if we can do this," she said. "I was just kind of worried about him and I was going to miss him, and long distance doesn't work, and I felt unafraid to just kind of walk away from everything, because I was going to miss this person, period, and I didn't want to let him go."

The couple settled into life in Kansas City with Claudia serving as Tomas's overnight caregiver, relieved by a nurse during the day. Her frequent trips out of town for work soon wore on the couple. "Every time I left it was very painful for me and for him," she said. "I had to leave him in the hands of somebody else. I had learned to take care of him all the time in the hospital. So at a certain point, you know, I just didn't want to leave him. I ended up taking a Certified Nursing Assistant course so I could learn how to take care of him and do all of the things I needed to do. I said 'I've had a good run at this job but I want to be home with you, then I'll have help in the afternoon, I'll take this on,' and it became a magical time, because we took care of all the medical stuff early, and then we just kind of, you know—he played video games, or watched movies or TV or listened to standup and music."

The "medical stuff" Claudia refers to was the daily routine of caring for her husband. "I would put the suppository in his rectum, and then I would empty his rectum of stool, and that was just once a day in the morning," she said, "and then the rest of the time he would just empty his urine into the bag from a Foley, and then I'd have to crush up his pills, and then every other day we'd kind of do a shower in the shower chair—so I'd get him in the lift, put him in the chair, and I'd roll him into the shower—and then we'd have appointments, we'd have to go to the VA for a psych appointment or a follow-up. That was mostly it."

Activism, of course, came to a grinding halt. Tomas's focus shifted to personal comfort and the new rigors of daily living. His world turned inward.

Even simple telephone calls became troublesome. Holding the receiver was one difficulty easily solved by speakerphone; managing to enunciate clearly was another matter entirely. It was very hard for friends and family to understand what Tomas was saying over the phone, and even harder, of course, to keep asking him to repeat himself. Those long phone calls with Eddie Vedder where Tomas could forget all his worldly cares suddenly became problematic. "After he came out of the coma, it was harder to have those conversations," said Vedder. "It would still be a two-hour conversation, but now it took two hours to cover what you would normally cover in about a half-hour of the old days." Young's new speech difficulties, compounded by Vedder's hearing loss—developed through two decades of performing on loud stages and recording at loud volumes—made any phone conversations between the two extremely tough. "It was *incredibly* difficult and really frustrating," Vedder recalled, "and I just wanted to—if there was *anything* I could have done—it just made me want to scream to the fucking high heavens with frustration when that happened."

Nathan Young returned to the United States from his second deployment to the Middle East in December, 2008. He had spent twenty-seven of his last thirty-eight months in Iraq. The last eight months of this most recent deployment saw Young again working as an infantry soldier, searching and clearing houses, "kicking in doors and doing a lot of patrols and crazy stuff," he recalled.

Ninety days after his return home, Nathan was finally discharged from the Army. "I got out in February 2009, and that's when the economy pretty much took a crap and I couldn't find a job," he said. Nathan was in no shape to find a job anyway, given what he'd just been through. "Every day we had to go out on patrol," he told me, sighing and pausing for several seconds, "so that second deployment took a toll on me mentally."

He moved in with his brother and began attempting to reacclimate to civilian life.

"I was on unemployment for a little over a year," Nathan said. "Mainly I just hung out with him. We sat back in his room and smoked pot and watched movies. . . . I was going through a rough time, just because my second deployment was pretty rough on me."

Still living in Chicago at the time, Cathy made sure her son had the necessary support during his transition to civilian life. "The first thing we did when he got back was to get him into the VA," she said. "Get him under a psychiatrist's care, get him medicine." That also meant getting him around other veterans. "From all of the work that I had done with veterans," she said, "everything that I had been through with IVAW and VFP and all of the veterans I've known, the most important thing for all of them was contact with other veterans. Because people that haven't been there don't know."

She was happy that Nathan was able to spend the time with his older brother. "I thought it was probably one of the best things for Nathan just to be able to live with Tomas and not have to worry about finding a job, and you know, just get . . . not crazy," said Cathy. The two brothers ventured out every now and then, including a trip in May to see Nine Inch Nails and Jane's Addiction at the Starlight Theatre. Tom Morello's band, Street Sweeper Social Club, opened the show, so Tomas and Nathan visited with Morello and Trent Reznor backstage. They also took a trip to Chicago, where they saw Pearl Jam on two consecutive nights at the United Center in August. Cathy and Timmy came along too for the second night, where Eddie Vedder played "No More" at Nathan's request. "When a soldier asks you to play this song, you play the fucking song," Vedder told the crowd, before apologizing to Timmy for the swearing.

They traveled further afield, too. One trip saw Nathan, Tomas, and Claudia take the van to Colorado. "We went out there looking for a place to live," Nathan recalled. "We were talking about living there."

Nathan wound up returning to Colorado in 2010, when Tomas's friend Garett, who worked for Veterans Green Jobs, found him work there. It was a short-lived position—"I was there for a couple of weeks, and it was pretty much slave labor," Nathan recalled. "I mean, seven twenty-five an hour, and living up in the back country digging out trails and . . . I did that for one week and said, no, I'm not doing that." But there was a silver lining: Nathan met his wife Amanda, an Air Force veteran, there. He moved out of Tomas's house and headed to south Texas with Amanda and went to college. The pair were married two years later.

When Secretary of Defense Leon Panetta participated in a flag-lowering ceremony in Baghdad on December 15, 2011, signifying the end of US involvement in the war in Iraq, Tomas Young was at home in Kansas City with Claudia. He didn't make any public statement marking the occasion. He remained passionately opposed to US involvement in Iraq, but his precarious health necessitated a focus on well-being and personal comfort rather than on activism.

"To be a paraplegic, deal with that," Cathy told local radio station KCUR a few years later. "And then wake up and you're quadriplegic . . . and you can't use your voice, which is what you were learning to use. So many people wanted him to speak, and he couldn't speak anymore." Speaking remained tremendously difficult for Tomas after the anoxic brain injury and remained a point of endless frustration for him.

"It was just *so* hard, and it hurt so bad that we lost one of the great antiwar activists of our time with that, 'cause it was much more difficult for him," said Vedder. "You know, something we always talked about—it was like a player talking about the big game—his goal, his World Series, the championship bout that he wanted was with Bill O'Reilly. He wanted to take him down, and I think he had gone through that—you know how politicians rehearse for a debate? He had practiced that debate in his head with Bill O'Reilly probably a thousand times, and we would go over it together, and he'd have me howling with laughter at how good he was, and how Bill O'Reilly wasn't going to stand a chance."

Tomas did continue to travel occasionally—he made a trip to Oregon at one point and also traveled to Atlanta to attend Wrestle-Mania with Riley Soden—but, as Soden said, "It was a lot of fun, but I could just see that the longer the trip, the more of a struggle it is for him. He just likes to be in that comfortable situation." Getting out was complicated and uncomfortable. More often than not, he opted to stay home.

Tomas and Claudia were married in a civil ceremony on April 20, 2012. "I always said I'd rather be dead than wed," Tomas told me with eyebrows raised, "and look at me now—twice married." Tomas chose the date—4/20—as a cheeky marijuana reference. The pair were married in a field behind the justice of the peace's office near their home in Kansas City, with the daughters of two friends serving as flower girls for the brief ceremony.

Both having been through previous marriages, neither of the pair felt it was particularly symbolic or important to get married. They wanted to tie the knot for other reasons. "We started hearing stories about caregivers who were shut out at the end—if their disabled partner or sick partner went to the ER or passed away, I'd have no rights," Claudia explained. Without being Tomas's legal partner, the fact that she'd been his full-time caregiver for four years would prove meaningless. "We were listening to the plight of many gay couples who—or a caregiver for a very extended period—have no rights, and are treated not only badly by the system but by families. So he did it to protect me. We had been through the wringer before with marriage and divorce, so we felt like we didn't need it, but we thought it would help me in the future when things get tough."

Chapter 11

Darkness

You know, you make your funeral arrangements before you get deployed.
He's like, 'Claudia, I was prepared every day to die, you're kind of ready, but
nobody's really ready to come back disabled.' Nobody ever thinks about that.

—Claudia Cuellar

Things did indeed get tough, and quickly. Less than two months after the wedding, Tomas began experiencing excruciating abdominal pain which would force him to spend most of the rest of 2012 in the hospital.

Tomas's digestive function had been gradually deteriorating over the past few years. Spinal cord injury patients are already prone to constipation and other bowel issues, and the marked decrease in his physical activity, combined with an increase in prescribed medications after the embolism and a series of increasingly frequent bladder infections, further slowed down his gut. "The bag is on his leg, and the line goes in his penis and up into his bladder," Claudia explained. "Then bacteria can actually creep up from the exterior to the interior, so then we'd have to take antibiotics, and the antibiotics are so harsh on his stomach. So from all the pills and the antibiotics over two to three years, he had more and more distension, he was

having more trouble passing stool, we were having to do more enemas, and laxatives, and milk of magnesia . . . we tried everything to
try to keep him moving."

The already small number of occasions on which Tomas did
venture out of bed decreased as the distension worsened. The more
sedentary he became, the more it compounded the problem.

Then the acute pain in his stomach began. Claudia recalled that
the pair "worked with it" for a month or so before they relented and
began what became a series of visits to the hospital. "He started the
revolving-door hospital visits at the VA in July," Claudia said. "They
would treat symptoms and release him."

The notion of a paralyzed individual experiencing severe pain in
an area below the level of the spinal cord injury—where they typically feel no sensation at all—is puzzling to both the casual observer
and the medical professional. However, a review of several studies
provided in *Wheeling and Dealing* indicates that Tomas's experience
with chronic pain is not atypical. "While the experience of chronic
pain is quite variable, most studies indicate that it does not dissipate
over time and is often unresponsive to pharmacological and surgical
interventions," the book reported. "The etiology and pathophysiol-
ogy of SCI-related pain are only partly understood. Most studies
report that this pain cannot be adequately conceptualized as either
a purely physiological or a purely psychological phenomenon."

No matter the cause of the pain, Tomas was desperate for some
relief. "I was in some really heavy pain, and I was asking for some
kind of painkiller," he said. "When I would go to the VA, they would
give me one dose of the narcotic painkiller Dilaudid in the emergency room and then they'd check me in to admit me, and when I
would have the pain problems again they'd tell me they couldn't give
me that [again] because it would slow down my stomach muscles
and I wouldn't be able to defecate. So I would be in pain and I
would say my pain was a ten, very severe, and they'd say, 'Oh, you're
lying, if it were that bad you would be screaming right now.' I was

like, 'I'm a soldier, we're not trained to whine.' And Claudia would say, 'You don't understand, he's not like that, he has a high tolerance for pain—just because you might be screaming your head off at ten doesn't mean he would be.'"

As the episodes continued, Tomas's visits to the VA became stressful and traumatic to the point that he'd have to take a Xanax before visiting their facility to keep the anxiety at bay. After one visit, when he'd been admitted for testing, he had finally had enough. "They would put what's called an NG tube which goes up my nose, down my throat and into my stomach, and it's connected to a suction device and the purpose is to suck the bad stuff out of my stomach," he said. "Well, the problem was, the VA and most hospitals have very dry air. I assume that's because moist air would make infections more frequent. So the air's dry, and this tube down my throat is making my mouth constantly dry, so I'd take a sip of water or a sip of Powerade. So they put it in one night and I said, 'So you'll take it out tomorrow morning?' And they said, 'Sure, absolutely.' But all this water and Powerade gets sucked up, just the same as the bile or whatever, and it would all go in this receptacle. And they would judge, based on what was in the receptacle, whether I could have the thing taken out of my nose or not. When I told them I was drinking water and Powerade, and that was why it was so full, and only a little bit of it was stomach stuff, and I felt fine now, they said, no, we're going to have to leave it in for another day. At that point I didn't know if it was punishment or actually medical, 'cause I felt fine and it stank of punishment, and I just felt I was being treated like a second-class citizen, so I called Claudia and I said, get to the hospital, I want to go AMA. Against Medical Advice. And so she showed up, and I had told the nurse what I was doing, and she said, 'Well that's just fine, I have other patients to take care of that want to be here, and if you don't want to, then that's fine with me.' She was a cunt."

When Claudia arrived, Tomas asked her for some paper towels and pulled the NG tube out himself before leaving.

The VA's reaction to Young's behavior was apparently to throw up their hands and say there was nothing further they could do to help him, a response which infuriated the couple. "The last time we went to the ER," said Claudia, "I said my husband was in pain, and the ER [doctor] callously looked at both of us and said, 'Based on my experience with repeated hospital visits, it looks like your next stop is going to be a skilled nursing facility.'"

"The admitting ER doctor said, 'You know, when we see people like this, that are in here so many times for the same thing, that we can't figure out the problem, they usually just get transferred to hospice care,'" Tomas added, "Which meant this one building where you just go to die."

It was a frustrating and fruitless cycle. Tomas, in pain, would go to the ER and, due to his sour relationship with the VA, end up leaving angry and frustrated beyond belief—and still in pain. The result was that Tomas didn't want to go to the VA, and the impression he got from the VA was that they didn't want to continue trying to treat him. "That's the thing," said Claudia: "He is suffering, he is in discomfort, he is in pain, and people question it, when it is the wish of every person to not suffer, not be uncomfortable, not be in pain. So there's just something that makes me sad that anyone would question him as an adult with all his faculties, a free man in a free society who has made the ultimate sacrifice."

There were undoubtedly occasions when Tomas was far from an ideal patient, but such behavior is surely understandable—expected, even—for someone who'd endured so much. Tomas said he became known at the VA as "Mister AMA." "Instead of criticizing him for that," said Claudia, "they should have said, well what would make a person who came here for help in the first place want to get out? But they're not looking at it in terms of helping human beings. They just kind of look at it as a case, not as a person. I mean they are overloaded as a system, so they're doing the best they can, but it just seems substandard for the sacrifices that have been made. It's like another broken promise. He was treated with such a measure of disrespect, and you know, just uncompassionate care."

"The VA was—is—one of the worst places to go in all of Kansas City," said Tomas in 2013. "It's just . . . the care I received, I felt like they were treating me like I was just another statistic, just a number, not a person."

Meanwhile, Tomas's digestive issues and abdominal pains continued. "We just kind of hit a wall where his digestive stopped functioning, and he was very distended," Claudia recalled. "He looked like a football was in there, it was just so big, because there was no movement." He also began experiencing pains in his chest. "I felt like I had a serious gas pain or something up here in my chest," he said. "It felt really bad."

Not ready to return to the VA hospital so soon after his recent traumatic experience, Tomas went to Saint Luke's North, which was only about fifteen minutes from his house. The experience at Saint Luke's was far better. "They fixed the pain in my chest," he said. "They gave me Dilaudid as I needed it, told me to press the call light every three hours and they would give me another dose. They said, yes it will slow your gut muscles, but to counteract that they gave me an antibiotic called erythromycin, which is designed to make the stomach muscles move. And I just thought, 'Why didn't the VA do that?' They did X-rays and they determined that I had some kind of problem in my stomach, I don't remember what, but they kept me there and admitted me. I had a doctor who would come and see me at ten-thirty on a Friday night, he'd come see me one Monday morning, and said, 'No, I think we're going to fix your problem,' and I'm thinking, 'Wow, I never got that at the VA, that kind of work ethic.' I was quite pleasantly surprised."

Tomas and Claudia were buoyed by the positive atmosphere. "We were at a private hospital and we felt like they were treating him better, and we trusted the situation more," said Claudia. The concept of a pain-free future didn't seem so farfetched anymore.

The medical team at Saint Luke's conducted further testing on Tomas's digestive system to try to isolate the cause of the distension and pain. "They could see from the testing that the transit time for his small colon was five hours and the large bowel was just kind of floppy and dead, so nothing was moving in there," Claudia recalled. "And that's what they thought the problem was—why I was in pain—because I had stool blocking it," added Tomas. The Saint Luke's team decided it would be necessary to remove Tomas's colon, which started a new series of decisions as to where the surgery should be performed. "Their surgeons [at Saint Luke's North] didn't want to perform the surgeries I needed, they wanted a bigger hospital," he said. "And the VA that I normally go to downtown has the second-best gastroenterology team in the country, but they didn't want to do it because all that they had done colostomies on was cancer patients, they had never done one on a spinal cord patient before, and so they didn't know what the effects would be." Tomas and Claudia faced similar reluctance when approaching both the VA medical centers in Saint Louis and in Leavenworth, Kansas. "Again, they have experience with cancer and with Crohn's and all this stuff, but they're not experienced with spinal cord injuries, so they didn't want to take the risk," said Claudia. "Plus," added Tomas, "I was known as 'Mister AMA' among the VA, so they said, 'Why would it matter if he was down here, he'd AMA anyway'—you know."

The surgery ultimately took place at Saint Luke's Hospital in downtown Kansas City in October 2012. Tomas had what is known as a colectomy, or the removal of his large bowel, followed by a colostomy, where the end of the colon is redirected to a surgically created opening in the abdominal wall. Tomas was actually given two stomas, or surgically created openings: The proximal stoma was connected to his upper gastrointestinal tract and drained his stool into a colostomy bag, which rested on his stomach. ("Because I had my large bowel removed, because it doesn't travel through there any more, the colon is where the water is removed from the fecal matter to make it look like stool, now it comes out as liquid," he explained.) The other stoma was the distal stoma (also known as a mucous fistula), which drained mucus and gases from the nonfunctioning part of his rectum.

About a week after the surgery, Tomas began the process of transitioning from feeding tube back to regular diet before gradually moving to solid foods. "I could do clear liquids and Jell-O and things like that, and when they finally got me transferred up to eat regular food, nothing would stay down," Tomas said. He was having trouble swallowing. "Their initial thought was that because I hadn't eaten for two and a half months, my throat needed time to reacclimate to swallowing," he said. "So I went to the VA, and they did what's called a swallow study, where they gave me cups of barium and a graham cracker, and they had an X-ray machine that followed the barium and food down to see exactly where the problem was, and the problem wasn't with my swallowing—the stomach opening had shrunk. And so we had to go get it dilated, or stretched out." Dilating his stomach opening worked for a time—he was able to eat soft foods such as oatmeal—but then "one day I was drinking some water and I noticed that it started to close up again," said Tomas. On another occasion, he tried eating a biscuit and "almost choked, so I decided to eat either soft things that slide down, or tube feeding was what I was going to do because I didn't like sitting here for three hours trying to dissolve the biscuit enough to where it would just slide down."

He said he was told that they could dilate his stomach again, but the problem would likely recur. "So I just said, forget it, I'll just do tube feedings. And apparently Claudia talked to some mother who had the same problem with their son and they'd done it so much that he was almost unable to breathe."

It was a momentous decision, and an indication of Tomas's mindset at the time. He elected to stop further efforts to correct his swallowing issues because he couldn't bear the discomfort and disappointment that came with those efforts. His desire to be left alone outweighed his hunger. Meanwhile, Claudia recalls, "he couldn't eat, and the dude's hungry, and the nurses are just outside the door talking about what they're going to have for dinner or lunch, or the potluck, or the pizza party. It was like a completely different world, like no consideration for the people in their rooms that are suffering."

Another complication soon surfaced. Tomas, weakened and underweight after his long bout with digestive problems, was a prime candidate for pressure sores. He soon developed one on his left hip. "He was malnourished for a while, because they couldn't figure it out," said Claudia. "And during that time, he just kept getting sicker and sicker because he couldn't keep down any food or nourishment. Jell-O and broth isn't going to build your body back. He lost a lot of weight. We would check his skin every day. . . . On a transfer, maybe, across the bed, it just—it tore his skin."

By December 2012, Tomas was back home after more than two months in the hospital. He was unable to eat by mouth, and fighting multiple pressure sores—another pressure sore had developed soon after the first. "I shifted [his body] to take pressure off of one hip to allow blood circulation to come and have it heal faster, and then that made another hole on the other side, because then I put more pressure on *that* one, trying to offload the other one," Claudia said. "You know, Christopher Reeve died of a sepsis from a pressure sore. He lasted ten years, he had the best of care, and he ended up dying from a simple sepsis from a pressure sore." Tomas now had a large pressure sore on each hip. A third pressure sore—on his tailbone—would soon develop.

Then, within just days of Tomas's return home, came a devastating blow. After all the hospital visits, the testing, the surgery and its attendant complications, the abdominal pain roared back. The debilitating colon surgery, while it addressed Tomas's distended gut and poorly functioning digestive system, had failed to stop his chronic pain. When the pain returned, it was no less excruciating than it had been before.

December and January were a blur of hospital visits because of the pain, because of repeated bladder infections, because of the pressure sores. "I couldn't keep him home and not in pain," said Claudia. "All we wanted to do was go home and be pain-free. That was kind of our goal. Because the hospital stays were just literally killing him. I mean, he was just so tired. Exhausted. Because of the bright lights, the beeping IV thing, you know. . . . And then to have blood draws done at like three or four in the morning, or they do vitals at one, I'm like, who can heal in a place like this? I know they need to get their labs, but don't patients need to rest? And so I'd have to fight to have a four- or five-hour span where they wouldn't come into the room to bug him so he could rest. All we wanted was the quality of life where we could go home and be pain-free."

Tomas and Claudia were distraught. They had hoped that better times lay ahead after the surgery, but those hopes had been quickly dashed. "He was supposed to come home, he was supposed to be healed by Christmas, he was supposed to be eating food, you know, working ostomy bag—fine," Claudia said, "but then it was like, nothing by mouth, boring pressure sores into his buttocks— three big, open sores, like the size of my fists."

The couple now faced an impossible choice: go back to the hospital for more testing and treatment, or stay home and suffer. Tomas had endured so much physical and mental suffering that he finally began showing signs that he couldn't take any more. "It was in December that I started seeing that thousand-yard stare—like a catatonic, very faraway look," said Claudia. "You know, when you look at a person and you just feel like they can go no further. I could see in his eyes—I looked at him and said, 'I don't know if you can take another hospital visit. I mean, it'll kill you.'"

Tomas, tired of trying new approaches or new procedures and being disappointed, wanted to be left alone. The prospect of hospice care—of opting out of further procedures, testing, and surgery and choosing simply pain management—became the most appealing option.

"They just want to keep doing procedures, surgeries, drugs," said Claudia of the medical system. "It's always like the next procedure, the next test, the next pill. And it seems like pain management under that system . . . the pills that they were giving him for pain weren't being absorbed in his gut and we had to kind of always plead our case with getting the right pain medicine. And so it seems in order to be able to have control over your own pain medicine, you have to peel over into hospice, because in a regular hospital situation, it's a very controlled . . . I don't know, like, there's people who are in pain and the establishment holds the medicine and they are very . . . you have to plead your case to them. There's something kind of dehumanizing about that."

The couple soon found that the process of moving to hospice, which required a doctor's approval, involved further pleading. "If you're not designated as terminal from cancer, it's very hard to get in," said Claudia. "And when we are saying that he's exhausted, that he's procedure-weary, he doesn't want to do more surgeries, doesn't want to do more pills, we want to be at home, we want to be pain-free, we don't want to die in the hospital, in the ER, or in a nursing home, the doctor's like, 'But he's not a typical hospice candidate because he's thirty-three.' But this is what happens when a country sends its poor sons and daughters to war. Broken bodies will be returned . . . and broken bodies, just like a diseased body, just like an aging body, will deteriorate over time."

Chapter 12

Deciding to Die

What good is living life if you're in pain all the time or sick all the time . . .
when there's no hope in sight, really?

—Tomas Young

By 2013, Tomas was seriously contemplating how to end his
life. Exhausted from the pain, the endless trail of hospital
visits, and the steady decline of his health, he decided that he had
finally had enough. Back when he was in middle school, his mother
had told him that suicide was "a permanent end to a temporary
problem," Tomas told me. "This," he said, referring to the decision
to end his life, "is a permanent end to a permanent problem."

Broaching this subject as an interviewer is a tough, uncomfortable task. During our first meeting, just before Tomas and Claudia's first wedding anniversary, I asked Tomas tentatively if he could
"speak a little bit more about what led to the decision to . . ."

"To end my life?" he offered as my voice trailed off. "Yeah," I
replied meekly.

"I'd thought about the idea for a little while," said Tomas, clearly more comfortable with the subject matter than I was, "and then
once all this happened, I just saw myself going further and further

into more pain, and just watching my body deteriorate over time, and I don't . . . I mean, technically I could live for a long time, but it's not a life that I want to live."

The fact that I was having a hard time asking the questions was nothing new to Tomas. Claudia had told me that her husband found it interesting that other people seemed to have more difficulty with the notion of him ending his life than he did. Tomas said he wasn't having a particularly hard time with the decision. "It's not as though I'm ending my life," he said, implying that his life was already over. "I'm ending my suffering. Because what good is living life if you're in pain all the time or sick all the time . . . when there's no hope in sight, really?"

"I'm at peace with my decision, because I know that when it happens, I won't feel any more pain or sadness or anything," he told me. "Of course I won't feel happiness or anything like that, but I won't feel *anything*—that'll be the ideal situation. I mean—if the soul exists, and I stay alive in some heavenly realm or hell . . . then I'll take my lumps. But I believe what I believe and I just think of it as a . . . forever nap."

Tomas added some conditions to the decision to end his life, centered on those he loved. He wanted to give friends and family notice before his death, to give them an opportunity to visit and say goodbye. "This was a fairer way to treat people than to just go out with a note," he said. He also wanted his loved ones to have no part in the physical act of ending his life. "I wouldn't be able to shoot myself or even open the pill bottle to give myself an overdose," he explained. "The only way I could think of doing it was to have Claudia open the pill bottle for me, but I didn't want her implicated." Cathy had already informed her son that she wouldn't help him end his life. "I had told him many times that I would never help him on his journey," she said, "because . . . how do I go on tomorrow? I still have another child to raise, and grandchildren, and—you know, how do I help you kill yourself and then I go on? I can't."

Another condition Tomas added to the list was that he didn't want his death to coincide with his young niece's upcoming second birthday. "I don't want the celebration of her birthday to be marred by the non-celebration of the day I die," he said. "I don't want the pallor of me dying on the same day as her birthday hanging over the festivities. She's the closest thing I have to a daughter. . . . I think the world of that little girl."

Not yet married for a full year, Young's plan was to celebrate his first anniversary on April 20 with Claudia and to complete the act of ending his life prior to his niece's birthday in June.

The days after he'd made the decision didn't get any easier. Tomas now faced the daunting task of informing his loved ones of his plans. He began with his mother. "He called me over, and I went over to the house, and he just started crying and said that he was just so tired," Cathy recalled. She'd moved back to Kansas City from Chicago after Tomas began experiencing his digestive issues and abdominal pain the previous year.

> He said, "I just can't do it anymore, and so I've decided to just . . . stop. Everything. Stop my feeding tube." We talked about it, and I told him how painful it was going to be, 'cause starvation and dehydration is one of the most painful forms of dying. And he just said, "It's no more painful than living." And I don't know, we talked about it for quite a while at length, and—you know, it's hard to say we had this conversation, because most average people can't wrap their head around having this conversation, but most average people haven't already arranged their son's funeral years ago. You know, that's the first thing you do when you send your sons off to war, you find out through them who they want to officiate, what music they want—that's something they do when they go off to Iraq. Most average people haven't spent every other day telling their son, you know, "You're not going to kill yourself—this is a permanent solution to a temporary problem." It wasn't like he had told me this and it was all a surprise. We had talked about it and talked about it and talked about it.

Cathy had been a rock throughout these nine years since To- mas had been shot and had weathered a tremendous amount of emotional stress. It was only recently that she had sought help. "For the very first time during all of that I spoke to a therapist," she said. "During the whole time I had never spoken to a therapist, never been on medication—and if anybody needs medication it's proba- bly me," she added with a chuckle. "But one of the things that the therapist said to me that really struck home and really helped me out was, he said, you go over there expecting a certain thing to hap- pen, whether it's going to be a bad time every time you see him, or you expect it to be butterflies and rainbows and unicorns, you know, and everything's going to be happy, and then you go over there and it's not. And he said, so what you need to do is not expect anything. You know—it is what it is—it's going to be what it is. And so for me, that was kind of a turning point."

Prior to this point, Cathy's visits with her son had become less frequent as the emotional toll increased. "You know, I did go through a time when my visits became fewer and farther be- tween," she said. "'Cause he didn't need me around, didn't want me around, kind of just wanted to sit in the dark and go through what he was going through. So when I came over I, you know, tried to be positive . . . but yeah, we did go through kind of a peri- od where Mom wasn't there every day. Because he didn't want her to be there every day, and that was breaking my heart, everything that was going on."

Cathy's impression that Tomas didn't want her around wasn't something that her son intended. On the contrary, he and Claudia told me that they felt increasingly lonely during this period and would have appreciated more company. But the few visits with family and friends that did occur during this period were often awkward and uncomfortable. Ultimately, neither scenario provided much comfort for Tomas. "I spend a lot of time sitting here in my bedroom, watching TV or sleeping," Tomas said at the time. "I have found—I don't know if it is the result of my decision or not—[it is] equally hard to be alone or to be around people. This includes my wife. I am rarely happy. Maybe it is because when I am alone all I have with me are my thoughts, and my mind is a very hazardous place to go. When I am around people I feel as if I have to put on a façade of being the happy little soldier."

Claudia, for whom staying away wasn't an option, tried coping in a different way. She found that studying Buddhist teachings provided a helpful lens through which to view the tragic situation she'd found herself in.* "I feel like they are really good instructions," she said. "There are very practical teachings on death and dying, and it's very close to the indigenous view that death is a part of the cycle of life, and because we're human, we have fears surrounding death, and we have to work with them. There's a base of teachings in Tibetan Buddhism that teach that ultimately the direct experience of being in the presence of someone who's dying is the ultimate privilege. And then a friend of mine who is a Tibetan lama, he's like, you know, you have to write everything down, because dying people know everything. Because if he's at peace and he's not afraid to die, his view is kind of unique."

But this perspective did nothing to diminish the devastating reality that her husband was close to death. "It certainly hasn't been easy," she said.

> It's been so much harder for him, and I certainly feel the guilt that I wish I could carry some of that burden somehow—but to have to bear witness to the suffering of the person you love most in the world, is something I never . . . I prepared myself for the possibility that he would die one day, and like I said, I followed the Christopher Reeve case very closely. When I met him in Chicago it was year four, and so I said, oh, well things are

---

* "When I moved in with Tomas," said Claudia, "when I arrived at the house the first time, the first thing is see is a Buddha on the front mantle. And so I walked in and I'm like, 'Hey, atheist, why is there a Buddha on your mantle?' To me, it was like, 'Whoa!' And he was like, 'Buddha wasn't a God, he was just a man. It's cool.'"

harder now with the embolism, so that was a reality, but I can see where we could have . . . I felt like we had some time, based on that case at least. Five, six years or more. I thought he would die one day maybe in his sleep at home—I mean, he never wanted to die in a hospital. But I certainly never imagined that I would have to bear witness to the deterioration over time. That's been so painful. Because if he feels helpless, I feel helpless as his caregiver. It's an impossible situation for someone to go through alone. So we have certainly been there for each other. . . . We are saying the things that two people that are in a relationship say to each other when they know there's only so much time left, so you start really talking about the important things, or expressing the true feelings that you have for each other.

When Tomas began notifying his friends, he encountered heavy-hearted support and acceptance. "It's the last thing I want to see, but I understand where his life is and I definitely don't want him to suffer," said Riley Soden. "And I don't want him to suffer *more* than I think our friendship will continue, you know? It's a weird line for me, but I know that we've talked about it in the past, and in the past he seemed to get over it easier. . . . You know, I'd just kind of say, 'Well, we won't deal with those people anymore,' or 'We won't have to go into that part of society, we'll just be us,' but now, the longer he goes on and the worse condition he gets . . . you know, it's hard to try to tell him that it's a bad idea."

Tomas broke the news to Roy McHugh over the phone. "We hadn't hung out in close to a year," McHugh recalled. "We talked to each other on the phone every now and again, and he was really depressed. It was just kind of hard to hang out with him. I'd go over to his house and I'd sit there for like two hours and we'd say like maybe a few words to each other. I felt bad because I hadn't hung out with him as much as I should, but . . . it wasn't 'cause we weren't friends, it was just 'cause it was kind of hard to take, you know?"

"He calls me up," McHugh continued, "and—that's kind of a hard thing to lay on someone—he tells me, 'I've decided that after some point in time I'm going to stop eating,' and . . . he never said 'take my life,' he just said, 'and that'll be it. I'll be . . . dead. I'll be gone.' And he doesn't believe in an afterlife or anything like that, so that's got to be scary, to think that you've got nothing else to go to." But Roy ultimately came to the same conclusion as the others. "I didn't want him to do it. I didn't know what to say to him, you know? Don't do it? 'Cause then you're just going to piss him off. So I told him, you know, whatever you need to do, you need to do. I came out to see him and we hung out."

Another of the close friends Young informed via telephone was Phil Donahue. "Tomas and Claudia called me, it was a Saturday, and he announced what he was going to do," Donahue remembered, adding that he told Young "something like, 'Tomas, this is your decision.'" He trailed off and admitted, "I don't know what I said. But I didn't cry until I hung up."

When he had composed himself, Donahue called Ellen Spiro, who, she recalled, "tried to wrap my head around it. And kind of came to the same conclusions that everybody close to him did, which is, you know, that Tomas has been through hell and back so many times that there's no way we could ever really understand what he's been through and that his choices are his choices."

Tomas's first public announcement of his decision came on February 1, 2013, during a Q&A session at a *Body of War* screening at a small theater in Ridgefield, Connecticut. Phil Donahue was on hand, while Tomas and Claudia appeared via Skype. "After my one-year anniversary with my wife," Tomas announced to the stunned crowd, "I will begin to wean myself off of food, and," he paused while Claudia, seated next to him, lowered her gaze. "One day . . . go away."

"This latest round of governing pain is just the proverbial straw that broke the camel's back," he explained. "I've been doing this for nine years. The last four of those have been post–pulmonary embolism/anoxic brain injury, where I lost a lot of dexterity and upper-body power." He shrugged slightly, adding, "And so I can't do things that I used to do even when I was first paralyzed. I'm so limited in the things that I *can* do on a daily basis that I feel essentially helpless, and I'm just tired of doing that every day."

The *Body of War* screening had been arranged before Tomas had told anyone of his decision. It was he who decided to publicly announce his decision there. "I didn't encourage him, obviously, in any way at all," said Donahue, who was surprised that nobody challenged Young's decision once he announced it. "I thought people would stand up and pray that he wouldn't—'Please, don't do this'—and they didn't. And I was very impressed by that. He has told me that there are people who love him that don't want him to do this, and he tries to gently say, 'Well, this is *your* wish.' It doesn't respect *my* wish. And if you think about it, he's right."

Perhaps too drained after the emotional meeting with his mother, Tomas didn't inform his closest sibling of his decision prior to the public finding out. Nathan's wife came across an article about Tomas's Skype announcement on the Internet and texted a link to her husband, who was at work. "He called me after he knew that I found out and said, 'Yeah, I wanted to tell you, but I just didn't have the chance to,'" said Nathan.

Cathy, who gave Tomas an earful when she found out, figured his reluctance to personally notify Nathan was because he knew he'd get no uplifting words of support from his brother. "It's not like his brother would say, 'Dude, I'm all about it—I respect your decision, I'll stand behind it,'" she said. "No, his brother would say, 'Really? You're an idiot. What are you talking about?' Yeah, Nathan's never been Tomas's spiritual guide." She laughed. "So he wasn't going to go to Nathan and get all sorts of uplifting help."

Nathan recalled his actual response as more along the lines of quiet, reluctant acceptance. "I mean, what are you going to say to him?" he said. "You know—'You shouldn't do it'? 'You should live

your life suffering the rest of your days'? Or . . . I mean, if it was me,
I wouldn't be able to do it. I wouldn't be able to live like that. So I
can't blame him. There was nothing I could say or do. I love him and
I'd like to see him stick around, but he's in agony and suffering the
whole time he's in this world."

The first person to interview Tomas after the announcement was
author and former *New York Times* foreign correspondent Chris
Hedges, now a columnist for the news website *Truthdig*. The resulting article, "The Crucifixion of Tomas Young," was posted on
Truthdig in early March.

"I felt relieved," Young told Hedges when asked how he felt
after making the decision. "I finally saw an end to this four-and-
a-half-year fight. If I were in the same condition I was in during
the filming of *Body of War*, in a manual chair, able to feed and dress
myself and transfer from my bed to the wheelchair, you and I would
not be having this discussion. I can't even watch the movie anymore because it makes me sad to see how I was, compared to how
I am. . . . Viewing the deterioration, I decided it was best to go out
now rather than regress more. . . . I will go off the feeding [tube]
after me and my wife's anniversary. . . . At first I thought I would
[just] wait for my brother and his wife, my niece and my grandparents to visit me, but the one thing I will miss most in my life is my
wife. I want to spend a little more time with her. I want to spend
a full year with someone without the problems that plagued my
previous [marriage]. I don't know how long it will take when I stop
eating. If it takes too long, I may take steps to quicken my departure.
I have saved a bottle of liquid morphine. I can down that at one
time with all my sleeping medication."

A few days later, Tomas aired his grievances in an open letter—
it was titled "The Last Letter"—to Dick Cheney and George W.
Bush. Tomas's full letter, posted on *Truthdig*, read:

I write this letter on the 10th anniversary of the Iraq War on behalf of my fellow Iraq War veterans. I write this letter on behalf of the 4,488 soldiers and Marines who died in Iraq. I write this letter on behalf of the hundreds of thousands of veterans who have been wounded and on behalf of those whose wounds, physical and psychological, have destroyed their lives. I am one of those gravely wounded. I was paralyzed in an insurgent ambush in 2004 in Sadr City. My life is coming to an end. I am living under hospice care.

I write this letter on behalf of husbands and wives who have lost spouses, on behalf of children who have lost a parent, on behalf of the fathers and mothers who have lost sons and daughters and on behalf of those who care for the many thousands of my fellow veterans who have brain injuries. I write this letter on behalf of those veterans whose trauma and self-revulsion for what they have witnessed, endured and done in Iraq have led to suicide and on behalf of the active-duty soldiers and Marines who commit, on average, a suicide a day. I write this letter on behalf of the some 1 million Iraqi dead and on behalf of the countless Iraqi wounded. I write this letter on behalf of us all—the human detritus your war has left behind, those who will spend their lives in unending pain and grief.

I write this letter, my last letter, to you, Mr. Bush and Mr. Cheney. I write not because I think you grasp the terrible human and moral consequences of your lies, manipulation and thirst for wealth and power. I write this letter because, before my own death, I want to make it clear that I, and hundreds of thousands of my fellow veterans, along with millions of my fellow citizens, along with hundreds of millions more in Iraq and the Middle East, know fully who you are and what you have done. You may evade justice but in our eyes you are each guilty of egregious war crimes, of plunder and, finally, of murder, including the murder of thousands of young Americans—my fellow veterans—whose future you stole.

Your positions of authority, your millions of dollars of personal wealth, your public relations consultants, your privilege and your power cannot mask the hollowness of your character. You sent us to fight and die in Iraq after you, Mr. Cheney, dodged the draft in Vietnam, and you, Mr. Bush, went AWOL from your

National Guard unit. Your cowardice and selfishness were established decades ago. You were not willing to risk yourselves for our nation but you sent hundreds of thousands of young men and women to be sacrificed in a senseless war with no more thought than it takes to put out the garbage.

I joined the Army two days after the 9/11 attacks. I joined the Army because our country had been attacked. I wanted to strike back at those who had killed some 3,000 of my fellow citizens. I did not join the Army to go to Iraq, a country that had no part in the September 2001 attacks and did not pose a threat to its neighbors, much less to the United States. I did not join the Army to "liberate" Iraqis or to shut down mythical weapons-of-mass-destruction facilities or to implant what you cynically called "democracy" in Baghdad and the Middle East. I did not join the Army to rebuild Iraq, which at the time you told us could be paid for by Iraq's oil revenues. Instead, this war has cost the United States over $3 trillion. I especially did not join the Army to carry out pre-emptive war. Pre-emptive war is illegal under international law. And as a soldier in Iraq I was, I now know, abetting your idiocy and your crimes. The Iraq War is the largest strategic blunder in U.S. history. It obliterated the balance of power in the Middle East. It installed a corrupt and brutal pro-Iranian government in Baghdad, one cemented in power through the use of torture, death squads and terror. And it has left Iran as the dominant force in the region. On every level—moral, strategic, military and economic—Iraq was a failure. And it was you, Mr. Bush and Mr. Cheney, who started this war. It is you who should pay the consequences.

I would not be writing this letter if I had been wounded fighting in Afghanistan against those forces that carried out the attacks of 9/11. Had I been wounded there I would still be miserable because of my physical deterioration and imminent death, but I would at least have the comfort of knowing that my injuries were a consequence of my own decision to defend the country I love. I would not have to lie in my bed, my body filled with painkillers, my life ebbing away, and deal with the fact that hundreds of thousands of human beings, including children, including myself, were sacrificed by you for little more than the greed of oil companies, for your alliance with the oil sheiks in Saudi Arabia, and your insane visions of empire.

I have, like many other disabled veterans, suffered from the inadequate and often inept care provided by the Veterans Administration. I have, like many other disabled veterans, come to realize that our mental and physical wounds are of no interest to you, perhaps of no interest to any politician. We were used. We were betrayed. And we have been abandoned. You, Mr. Bush, make much pretense of being a Christian. But isn't lying a sin? Isn't murder a sin? Aren't theft and selfish ambition sins? I am not a Christian. But I believe in the Christian ideal. I believe that what you do to the least of your brothers you finally do to yourself, to your own soul.

My day of reckoning is upon me. Yours will come. I hope you will be put on trial. But mostly I hope, for your sakes, that you find the moral courage to face what you have done to me and to many, many others who deserved to live. I hope that before your time on earth ends, as mine is now ending, you will find the strength of character to stand before the American public and the world, and in particular the Iraqi people, and beg for forgiveness.

The publication of Tomas's last letter led to a huge amount of media attention and brought Tomas's plight home to tens of thousands of observers worldwide. "I thought it was the most scathing and accurate indictment of war that's been written since the Vietnam era," Tom Morello told me later. "Tomas speaks with a singularly authoritative voice—as a soldier, as a paralyzed veteran, as an American who's looked this war dead in the eye, and is willing to call the perpetrators of the war what they really are, and that is war criminals. The intellect and the wit and the weight of his words in that letter are really inspiring to me. It's no surprise to me that that letter had the global impact that it did. I sometimes think he gets discouraged about the value of his activism, and what it may or may not have accomplished in the past and what it could accomplish in the future. I'll be the first to say I don't have to live in his body, so I've tried to rein in my selfish impulses to want him to be alive for many more years so that we can fight many more causes, shoulder to shoulder, and play many more shows with his face looming above in theaters very dramatically like a renaissance painting [laughs]. But at the same time I think that the weightiness of that letter and the impact that it had is . . . really lays bare how important Tomas Young is, how important his message is, and how important he is as a person."

Mixed in with the support Young received as a result of his letter was a sizeable amount of criticism and second-guessing of his decision. "There have been two people who wrote me letters saying, 'Don't kill yourself, that only lets the Bush and Cheney regime win if you kill yourself,'" he said. "I just want to write back to them, 'Yeah, you try to be paralyzed for nine years—or be paralyzed for four years, and then become more paralyzed in the middle of that, and spend the last five years in an electric wheelchair 'cause you can't do shit. We'll see how . . . 'Bush has won.'"

In addition, Tomas received emails and even knocks on the front door from religious people trying to save his soul before he ends his life. "They've tried to . . . not sway me from my goal," he said, "although there has been a little of that. The majority of those people tell me that before I go, I need to read the Bible and accept Jesus or Allah as my savior or I'm going to hell. They don't try to stop me from doing this, they just tell me that if I don't accept their version of the truth, then I'm going to forever burn in hell. But as my great secular hero Mark Twain said, 'Go to heaven for the climate and go to hell for the company.'"

Young ultimately viewed the criticism and second-guessing as disrespectful, given the pain and misery he'd endured over the past decade. "All they see is the person in the wheelchair," he said. "They don't understand that I can't control my bladder so I have a catheter inside my urethra, that I pee into a bag that has to be emptied, and I defecate into a bag. It's no life that I would wish on anybody but if someone were similarly situated, I mean had the same problems that I do, I wouldn't fault them at all if they made the decision that I made."

But the majority of feedback Young received as a result of his "Last Letter," as well as the publicity surrounding his decision to die, was supportive and positive. It took him by surprise. It also gave him sufficient pause to defer his decision to end his life. It reminded him that he had a purpose.

As Cathy put it,

The biggest reason that everything turned for him was that everyone just reached out, and everyone was so compassionate and everyone was, you know, "You have something left to say," and I think for Tomas, for a good long time that's been important for him to be able to have a voice in all of this. And . . . to go through everything, his body was degrading so fast, and he just was so sick, and he just couldn't see any light at the end of that tunnel. That was such a huge part of it, and then, 'cause he was going to take his own life—or just stop, you know, I didn't really look at it that he was going to take his own life, he was just going to stop working so hard to stay alive—so many people reached out to him to tell him how much he meant to them, and how special he was, and that he still did have a voice and that everybody cared about him, and I think that was a huge part of it. You know, Tom Morello did the benefit concert here, and . . . I think things like that really had a huge effect, and he felt like people did care, and it wasn't just me and Claudia and Nathan that cared, and I think that was a big part of it, and I think part of it was that he had just gone through the colostomy, and his health improved. He was not fighting the bowel issues so much, which was such a huge part of his everyday life.

Chapter 13

Letting Go, Embracing Life

He is a hard person to look at when we go out, because he represents our recent mistakes as a country, as a collective. What we let happen.

—Claudia Cuellar

I t's August 2013, three months since the tribute show, and I'm back in Kansas City to visit Tomas. It's a scorching hot, sunny day. Everywhere you look there is coverage of today's milestone: the fiftieth anniversary of Dr. Martin Luther King Jr.'s "I Have a Dream" speech in Washington, D.C. Aside from Tomas's van, the only other car in the driveway as I pull up is an old Volvo belonging to one of Tomas's nurses. I knock on the front door a few times and eventually let myself in, assuming everyone is in the bedroom at the back of the house.

The living room is quite bare. The couches are gone. Peaches, Tomas's golden retriever, who has been cared for by friends and family for the past few years, ambles across the hardwood floor to greet me. This is the first time I've seen a dog in Tomas's home, and it's a welcome sight. I walk past what used to be the Hunter S. Thompson room; now it's housing someone's belongings, back to being a guest room.

I knock and enter Tomas's bedroom. Claudia, Tomas, and John, the nurse, are gathered there, watching a replay of the full speech on CNN. Tomas says a polite hello, but he is intently watching the speech, so I find a seat and quietly watch too.

I look around and notice some changes since last time. There's a framed poster of Chicago Bears great Walter Payton on the wall that I don't recall seeing before. When I glance over at Tomas I notice that there's no pain pump next to his bed, nor any tubes to deliver his liquid dose of Dilaudid.

Once the speech is over, I learn that Tomas no longer uses the pain pump because the Dilaudid was losing its effectiveness. "We had to keep increasing the dose," Claudia explains. "He would keep plateauing, and he would start feeling pain again." More and more frequently, the hospice had to come in and adjust the dose administered by the pain pump. Eventually they decided to try a different approach. "They took me down off the Dilaudid and switched to fentanyl," Tomas says. When he looks at me, I notice that his eyes appear a little livelier and brighter than I'm used to. "What you normally do when you switch someone over on pain medicines," he continues, "is to take that dose of Dilaudid and halve it, and give that much fentanyl, although my doctor took half that dose of Dilaudid and then took another 25 percent off, so I was getting 75 percent less medicine than I was on the Dilaudid. So my body went through horrible withdrawals."

One Sunday evening just a few weeks ago, Tomas—who already has breathing issues due to the scar tissue in his lungs and from being a longtime smoker—began suffering severe shortness of breath and a rapid heart rate. Claudia rushed him to the emergency room. "I thought he was having a heart attack," she says. "They didn't say what might happen when switching to the new pain medication. . . . But if we had any inkling it would cause trouble we wouldn't have rushed to the ER, because we were thinking he was dying, so the doctor had to come here and apologize, because the hospice agency director felt like it was wrong, too." Despite the apology, Claudia and

Tomas wanted a new doctor. "I was so angry," Claudia recalls, "and I said, I don't want to work with a person like this."

The request to change doctors was granted. The new doctor took Tomas off the fentanyl, using methadone in its place. "They just worked it out where I was taking 30 milligrams of methadone three times a day, which the doctors and nurses say is an extremely high dose," says Tomas. "But it handles everything," Claudia adds.

The methadone is administered in pill form—three pills, three times a day. The pills are crushed up, mixed with a little water, and administered through his feeding tube, just like his other medications. "And now if I have added needs," Tomas resumes, indicating a bottle of morphine "that I give by eyedropper that I put in through my feeding tube for breakthrough pain. And if I get horrible, really bad pains I'm supposed to call the hospice."

This methadone/morphine combination has proven remarkably effective. "I'm virtually painless and I feel fine," Tomas tells me. When I remark that his current state would not have been considered within the realm of possibility just a few months ago, he nods in agreement and says, "Right." Claudia adds that, as always, they are proceeding with caution. "It seems to be working," she says, "but you know, with transitions it always seems to be a tricky process."

Summarizing his current health issues, Tomas tells me that his chronic abdominal pain is virtually gone. The pressure sores have also mostly filled in. The digestive issues are no longer a problem, given the surgery of ten months ago. Tomas's chief health concern today is the congestion in his lungs. "I have constant breathing problems, whether it's from smoking or the fact that I have had a lot of scar tissue in my lungs from various things," he says. "I may have to switch doctors again because this second one doesn't want to give me a bronchial antibiotic."

Back in April, when we first met, I wasn't even sure Tomas would be alive just a month later. Now, he's actually looking forward:

his long-deferred plans to move to Portland are back on. I ask him about his outlook today. "I'm just ready to go until it becomes too unbearable," he says, "because I've gotten kind of used to this girl and I don't want to say bye to her until I have to say bye to her. Plus," he adds, raising his eyebrows in mock earnestness, "I preordered the PlayStation 4 which will be coming out in November and a few of the video games, and look, I don't want to waste. . ."

But Claudia cautions that this newfound stability with Tomas's health is tenuous. "We've achieved a level of thrive under these conditions for now, and when he talks to people they say he sounds great, and I say, well he's already had an embolism," she says. "It's like riding the edge of not knowing and not getting too comfortable that he's doing good or not doing good, and so it's a roller coaster, it's hard. Every day is different."

I nod in agreement with Claudia, but add that I feel like some of the clouds have lifted since April. You don't make decisions to move or think about the future if you don't have a somewhat positive outlook. "Right," Tomas nods, adding that the prospect of moving to Portland is also lifting his spirits: "If I didn't have the option of Portland and no ability to get there, I'd be in a completely different mindset."

I ask Tomas about how the approaching relocation to Portland came about. He says it all started when he visited the area a couple of years back—after the embolism, but before the abdominal pain issues began—with Claudia and Riley Soden. "I just fell in love with the place and decided that's where I was going to move," he says. But the plans were shelved while he spent several months in and out of the hospital fighting abdominal pains.

Claudia explains that they still wanted to go to Portland in January 2013, after the surgery to remove Tomas's colon. They were attracted by the physical climate, a friendlier political climate, and legal medical marijuana. Finally, they were attracted to Oregon because it has an assisted-suicide law.* "Here you have to starve to death over time, and I have to watch it, and it just seemed barbaric," Claudia says. Taking Tomas to Oregon would allow him a more humane method of ending his life. "I was literally wanting to take him there to die, but he was too sick to transport, there was no way." So, again, the plan was shelved.

Now the move is back on because Tomas's health is the best it has been all year. "He's stabilized where he's not on the pain pump any more. We're doing methadone three times a day. Finally, after a lot of hits and misses with the doctors, they finally found a medicine that is handling the pain, so he's stable and he's good."

And, Tomas adds, "I don't have a giant pack to lug around everywhere I go."

The experiences of the past several months had also given the couple a live-in-the-moment mindset. "He was ready to die and I accepted him being ready to die—I had to," Claudia says. "So I had to contemplate his death, he contemplated his own death . . . so it's almost like you die by doing that. You're not afraid of anything anymore. So I think under normal circumstances, someone could look at us and say why would you move to Portland? It doesn't seem very practical. And I say, all I have to do is get him out there and get a roll-in apartment and we're good. You know, house, mortgage payment . . . I mean, I'll send them the keys, I don't care. I'm not worried about anything but getting him out there. So there's a certain 'no fear'—we felt responsible to other people, responsible to the

---

* Oregon was, at the time, one of only three states with an assisted suicide law. The Death with Dignity Act, passed in 1994, states that "a competent adult Oregon resident who has been diagnosed, by a physician, with a terminal illness that will kill the patient within six months may request in writing, from his or her physician, a prescription for a lethal dose of medication for the purpose of ending the patient's life." If the request is approved (after review by a second doctor) the patient must wait at least fifteen days and make a second oral request before the prescription may be written. The law also specifies that this process will "not have an effect upon a life, health, or accident insurance or annuity policy."

system, to the way things are, and now we don't have to follow any rules. So instead of going to die, we're going to live."

I wondered how Cathy had taken the news that her son was moving so far away from her. "You know, I didn't take it personally at all," Cathy said. "It wasn't about getting away from me, it was about getting away from Kansas City. And we talked about it, and it was just, they had medical marijuana, it was more of a different kind of person up there, more of the kind of people that Tomas likes, you know, more free-spirited, that kind of person, and Portland—you know, we used to watch the show *Portlandia* all the time and just laugh. He's been to the Pacific Northwest quite a few times and enjoyed it, and lived in Idaho, and I never, not for a minute felt like he was going up there to get away from me or anything like that at all. Yeah—sure, for a minute and a half, it hurt my feelings, sure, a little bit, but—he was going to kill himself a month ago. You know? And now he wants to move to Portland? Fuck yeah! Move to Portland!"

At this point, the plan is pretty well established. They're going to fly Tomas on a charter to Portland (a friend has pledged a free flight). Claudia is in the process of finding a suitable "roll-in" apartment. They'll figure out what to do with the house in Kansas City after trying out life in Portland for a few months. In the meantime, Tomas's nurse, John, will house-sit and take care of Peaches. He has already moved into the guest bedroom. "I just want to get him out there and we'll figure it out," says Claudia. "The whole idea is for him to get out there and enjoy it. He's doing well now, you know—I don't know if we've got a day or ten years, but I'm going to move forward with what we've got today."

I tell Tomas that I saw the photo he posted on Twitter of himself and Everclear front man Art Alexakis at a recent show. In it, Tomas has a broad smile on his face, the broadest I've ever seen. Plus, it was encouraging to see that he'd managed to get out of the house. "We weren't able to stay long," Claudia says. "We don't get to go out as much as we used to. . . . We used to go out two or three times a week, now it's like once a week, if that. Like, him getting in the chair and spending any time in the chair is just . . . he's in the bed all the time, which before it wasn't like that. And we'd eat together and we'd go to concerts, but now it's like, once in a while we can get out. So he's much more housebound now than he ever used to be."

Tomas begins to wheeze. Claudia gives him three cough assists and then leaves the room. He tells me they'll be on their way to Portland "hopefully by the end of September," or as soon as Claudia can get the logistics—new apartment, shipping of essentials, hospice care arrangements, and so on—set up. "I mean, I'd help," he says, "but talking to me on the phone for the first time is, let's say, difficult, due to my stroke."

I tell Tomas that I watched a film he recommended, *The Intouchables*. It's a French film—a true story—about a wealthy quadriplegic who hires an abrasive criminal character as his caregiver. The seemingly incongruous pair turn out to be a perfect match. I comment that I've read that an English-language version of the film is in production. "I'd go see the English version, just so people could go, 'Look—there's one of them!'" Tomas quips. He says he liked "the interaction between the caretaker and the patient." He asks for a cigarette. I pull one from the pack, place it between his lips, and light it for him as he takes a draw. I tell him I liked the fact that the caregiver didn't pity the disabled man at all, something the patient actually wanted. Another thing that stuck with me was the way he described his "phantom" pains—"I feel like a frozen steak thrown onto a red-hot grill."

"I don't feel that pain," Tomas says. I add that I remember him telling me that his pain was like someone with a steel-toed boot kicking him in the stomach. "Yeah, it was really bad." He still gets random pain at various locations, such as "when I was in the hospital for something else, for like a weekend two or three months ago, my legs just started to hurt. I was like, 'Why are they hurting so bad?' For like ten, fifteen minutes, they just *burned*."

Tomas says he still suffers from significant pain whenever he sits in his wheelchair for a time. "Yeah, when I get up and spend a fair amount of time in my chair, my upper back and neck just starts hurting really bad, it just shoots out." He also still has violent leg spasms at night when he's sleeping. Brie used to sleep in a different bed because of this, as does Claudia now, because "she's worried that I might hit her accidentally." He continues to suffer from severe stomach spasms, like the one that caused him to flip backward in his wheelchair and hit his head on the concrete driveway.

One point driven home by *The Intouchables, The Diving Bell and the Butterfly*, and my time with Tomas is that a spinal cord injury can leave the individual feeling like a static object in an animated world: watching visitors come and go while you, in your broken body, remain immobile in bed, alone again with your thoughts. "I've grown as used to that as I think you can," Tomas says. "I've grown to where I like my time alone. Sometimes it's fifteen minutes, sometimes it's an hour. Then I will smoke, or smoke weed, or lay here. . . . It's not the easiest thing you can get over, but you can get to a place where it's normal. It's your new normal."

I ask if he gets lonely. Does he wish he had more time alone, or does he wish he had someone to talk to more often? "No, I . . . Claudia talks *plenty*," he says, with eyebrows raised. "And we talk a lot, and then I have time to be by myself. I feel that I have a pretty good balance as far as that goes."

He doesn't seem to have ever really clicked with another person with a similar injury. When I ask about this, he mentions a fellow Missouri veteran with a spinal cord injury who contacted him about six months ago. "He heard about my story and asked if he could send me some stuff along in a package, and immediately a red light went off. I said, 'Yeah, you can send me a package of anything you want, just as long as Christ is not involved in that package,'" he says. "Then he wrote me back this big long missive about Jesus and how he saved his life—*all right, dude*." But the contact did prove beneficial, as the veteran made Tomas aware of an herbal supplement that is supposed to help prevent urinary tract infections. "I started taking that and in the past six months I haven't had a UTI, knock on wood," he says.

Tomas is starting to fall asleep as I'm talking to him. He is reluctant to talk about himself and tires of the subject relatively quickly. Preparing to end the interview for the day, I shift to a lighter subject: sports. I ask if he's watching much baseball. "Not a lot," he responds, perking up noticeably at the change in subject. "I'm playing a lot of video games. Today *Madden 25* came out, and it's a pretty wild game. I am the Chiefs, with a few upgrades at certain positions."

"Quarterback?" I ask. He nods. "RGIII is my quarterback. Calvin Johnson, A.J. Green and . . . who else . . ." He says he's a fan more of players than teams. "I was a Rod Woodson fan, so I loved Pittsburgh. Then he retired, and I became a Peyton Manning fan, so I follow him now. People say, 'Oh, you're a Broncos fan.' No, I'm a Peyton Manning fan. And I'm a Robert Griffin III fan, you know, so—whatever he does. I just like the game and I like players. And when I was able to walk, I would be watching football, then go outside and try to find some people and play football. When I got paralyzed, watching football makes me want to go on PlayStation and play football."

I mention the Walter Payton poster on the wall. Tomas points out a faded signature on the poster and explains that it was a gift from Eddie Vedder. "That Walter Payton poster there was Eddie's when he was ten years old. It was signed by Walter Payton and Eddie had it when he was a kid, and now it's hanging up on my wall," he says proudly. "He just sent it to me along with—somewhere in there—is the Captain America helmet from *Easy Rider*." I look on the shelf behind me, and, sure enough, there's a vintage Peter Fonda stars-and-stripes motorcycle helmet.

The mention of Vedder's name reminds me that Cathy told me Vedder had wanted to get Tomas out to Hawai'i to go surfing a few years back. Tomas doesn't remember anything about such a discussion, but says he'd like to give it a try. I ask if any of his physical therapy involved working in a pool. "No—no water," he says. "What I'd really like to do is learn how to scuba. My GI doctor is a scuba diver and deep sea diver and he showed me pictures of like sea turtles that he took underwater and all this stuff . . . wow, that's cool."

Tomas is exhausted, done for the day. I leave him in peace so he can take a nap, and I go out back. It's hot—a stifling, 95-degree late-summer day. The kind of weather Tomas won't miss when he gets to Portland. The tiny backyard is overgrown, thick with weeds several feet high. A small fence separates this overgrowth from a soccer field that leads up to a school behind the house.

That night, I sleep on a bed in Tomas's basement, directly below his bedroom. His old manual wheelchairs sit folded against the wall. A stack of *Body of War* movie posters lies on a nearby table. I wake every few hours as I hear Tomas himself awake in his bedroom above me, talking softly to Claudia, asking for a cough assist, a cigarette, or a bottle of water.

When I enter Tomas's bedroom the next morning, I explain that I want to talk to him about the shift that's taken place since we first met just five months ago. I tell him that I couldn't see the Tomas I'm talking to today writing "The Last Letter," and ask if the act of writing it perhaps helped him let go of some anger and resentment. "It was a cathartic letter in a lot of ways," he responds, nodding. "It got out a lot of the demons. It let me say, even though I couldn't say it directly to them, what I wanted to say to them, so yeah, I got a lot of shit off my chest as they say."

Tomas even seems to have forgiven George W. Bush somewhat, as evidenced by his comments during a recent interview with *Huffington Post Live*. "I think it was something about George Bush is a basically good person—he was just easily manipulated by Cheney and Wolfowitz, and that he's basically a good guy and he's upset that he's not liked so much and I hear that him and Cheney have a very limited relationship," he says. I note that I was surprised at these comments, to which Tomas responds, "I still hate Cheney and Wolfowitz with a vengeance, but although I hate what he's done, I don't hate George Bush the man."

While the anger has subsided a little, Tomas's views regarding the Iraq war remain intact. "I'd like to think there is no real difference," he says. "I mean, I still feel the same way politically and ideologically about that presidency and their decision to send hundreds of thousands of poor men and women to possibly die without really . . . as Bill Maher so succinctly said it right after we had gone to war, he said, 'A group of men operating out of Saudi Arabia, Pakistan, Afghanistan, and Iran comes up with a plan to fly planes into the World Trade Center, and we went to Iraq? So of course we go to Iraq.'"

During the long drive to Kansas City to visit Tomas, I listened to an audiobook about Buddhism, a major tenet of which is letting go of the past and living in the now. I mention this to Claudia one day when Tomas is napping, and ask her if Tomas's experiences have led him to a state of living in the now. She agrees and says, "He's not focused on the pain anymore, the way we were most of last year. So I think if that's out of the way, then he feels like he has a certain ability to enjoy life." She cites "his appreciation of the miracle of every moment—just like he really appreciates having the ability to play video games and listen to music." And spend time with a loved one, I add. Another example she provides: "He loves Kool-Aid. Like the little packets with the sugar, Kool-Aid, 'cause he can't drink much else—he can't do fizzy drinks any more, he just loves the Kool-Aid in a way like a little kid would, you know. He really appreciates it."

When I ask Tomas about his present mindset, he responds: "I've said at various times over the past few months that however you want to live your life, whatever makes you happy, do that. If that's living just for you and not worrying about anybody else, just living to watch TV, play video games, and nothing else, then do that. If helping other people and donating all your time and money to charity makes you happy and fills you with joy, do that. But do what you want to do, because nobody has any idea when they're going to die or become unable to do the things that you could do yesterday. So do whatever you want to do while you can still do it. I decided to do whatever I want to do till I can't do it anymore."

What is it that you want to do, I ask—what are the most important things to you now? "Being around Claudia, playing video games, being comfortable," Tomas says. "Claudia and personal comfort are the two driving things in my life."

I ask if activism is important to him anymore. "It is," Tomas responds, "and what I feel most worst about is I see all the marching on TV for better voting rights and for women's health care and for justice, equal justice for African Americans, and I used to be able to go out and march and . . . but now it would get too hot, or I'd get sick, or I'd have to go back home and do a feeding . . . so I'd like to but I can't."

He says he's looking forward to living in an area where there are more like-minded people. "Garett said the reason he lives in Colorado as opposed to Oregon,'cause he thinks the same way I do, is because he likes going out there in Colorado and having someone scream at him why he's wrong, and you don't get a lot of that in Oregon," he says, "and I don't *want* a lot of that!"

"What else are you looking forward to in Portland?" I ask.

"Looking forward to seeing more weed stores and liquor stores than churches."

Chapter 14

A Visit to Portland

It just feels like a lot of weight's been lifted off. We feel like we're being embraced again by culture and by people who are more like us, and we don't feel so alone.

—Claudia Cuellar

It's a beautiful sunny spring day in downtown Portland. It's been six months since I've seen Tomas, who lives in a third-floor loft here. The art museum sits nearby, next to a tree-lined park; the Willamette River lies just a few blocks away.

When Claudia opens the door, Peaches rushes out to greet me. So much for leaving the dog in Kansas City. Claudia is surprised to see me; some wires must have been crossed at some point during our communications, but she ushers me in anyhow. She hurries over to help Tomas put a T-shirt on.

I stand in the entranceway, just out of sight of Tomas, and look around. It's a compact, single-room loft, already piled with artwork and books, as was the house in Kansas City. There's a large dark sheet over the picture window, but it's still quite light. And another thing: I don't smell cigarette smoke.

Claudia quickly returns and escorts me back to see Tomas. His hospital bed is set up between the kitchen counter and the apartment's picture window, a Batman poster on the wall behind him and another on the wall facing him. A TV sits on a stand at the foot of his bed, an assortment of miniature comic-book-character figures arranged below it. He's had a haircut—his hair is still longish, but it's now short enough to stick up. He may have put on a few pounds. His eyes aren't as dark, his cheekbones less prominent. All of this combines to give him a more youthful appearance, more in keeping with his thirty-four years. When I look at his face now, for the first time I can see the Tomas Young of *Body of War*.

Claudia hands me a bottle of water and takes a seat at a nearby table, looking at her laptop but listening to our conversation. Tomas tells Peaches, pawing at him from beside the bed, to lie down. I ask him how the move to Portland went; he grimaces and says, "That would be a question for Claudia—she drove."

Claudia chimes in, explaining that the initial plan was for her and Tomas to fly, while a friend had offered to drive a U-Haul truck with all their belongings, hospital bed, and so on and meet them in Portland. However, their friend backed out late in the game, forcing them to reconsider. They wound up enlisting John, Tomas's caregiver in Kansas City. Since John was supposed to be watching Peaches, too, they opted just to make the trip in the van and bring her along.

So Claudia drove the van 1,800 miles with Tomas and Peaches on board, while John followed in the U-Haul. After the first leg—600 miles to Denver—they stayed at a hotel. Transferring from van to wheelchair and from wheelchair to standard hotel bed was enough of an ordeal for Tomas that he asked if they could just drive the remaining 1,200 miles without overnight stops, just shorter breaks.

So they scrapped their plans to spend the second night in Boise and drove straight through. "We barely slept," Claudia says. "I don't know, honestly, how we got here." Upon arriving in Portland, she and John unloaded the hospital bed, maneuvering it into the elevator and up into the apartment so Tomas could finally rest in relative comfort.

Surprisingly, Tomas says he endured the ride with relatively few issues. Maybe his anticipation of the destination helped him cope. "I could recline," he points out. "I was just getting"—he jostles his upper body around like he's in a car going over bumps. He points out that the alternative, airline travel, is hard for a disabled person, anyway—the trip through security is often degrading and painful, and when he's traveled in the past, his wheelchair has often sustained damage when they stowed it. "When I flew with my manual chair, I'd get it and something would be loose, or barely hanging on, or missing," he says.

Tomas is speaking more rapidly and is more animated than I've seen him before. He's also pulling on an e-cigarette. He was induced to quit smoking by his new apartment's no-smoking rule and hasn't smoked in months. His breathing sounds infinitely better; I didn't see Claudia give even one cough assist during my entire visit.

He tells me he's no longer on hospice care. And, he says, "the doctor at the VA tells me they're going to try to find a way to get me back to eating—I would look forward to that, because [during a previous visit] . . . there was a little restaurant here that we ate at that had Reuben sliders, and I was like, *woooow!*" He's upbeat and quick with his verbal jabs today. When I ask him if he's getting out much, he jokingly tells me to call his mom, then says in a nagging, nasal voice, *"Are you eating your greens? Are you getting out much?"*

I ask him how the VA care he's received here has been so far. "It's like a person who is steadily going blind doing target practice," he says. "Sometimes they hit and take a good shot, and sometimes they miss completely and think they hit it." Which doesn't exactly sound like a ringing endorsement of the Portland VA until he adds, "Back in Kansas City, it was like a *completely* blind man taking target practice. They just aim, and when they hit, it was a pure accident and luck."

"The quality is better here," he concedes. "It's just . . . it's like comparing really bad apples to really bad oranges."

He's still on the same morphine/methadone combination and is essentially pain-free, "if I don't go too long without it. If I accidentally miss the time to take it by three or four hours, my body has a very unpleasant way of reminding myself that I didn't take the pain medicine."

Claudia, listening in from the front of the apartment, chimes in that Tomas's methadone dose has gone up. He's now on 40 milligrams, three times a day. I ask if he finds himself needing much of the morphine, which is for breakthrough pain. "I use it more on the nights that I choose not to take my sleeping pills, because I like to take a physical break between the times that I take the sleeping pills, so that their efficacy doesn't go down," he says. "So on the nights that I don't take the sleeping pills, I take extra morphine. It seems to help me sleep."

One of the attractive features of moving to the northwest for Tomas was the fact that medical marijuana is legal in Oregon. He explains that he has a "green card" that allows him to purchase— and even grow—marijuana to be used for medical purposes. He's duly impressed with what's available here. "It really is unbelievable," he says. I ask if the quality was better here than in Kansas City. "Here, you get to pick what you want," he says, "and that is much better. So the quantity of quality goods is higher."

I notice a container of chocolate milk on the tray near Tomas, which prompts me to ask if he's still taking nutrition solely through the feeding tube. "I drink chocolate milk sometimes," he says. "There's a protein chocolate milk down in the store beneath us—but they've been out for the past few days—and that stuff is enhanced by extra protein, and so that works also. Because the tube feed, it gives my body all the nutrients and everything, but it doesn't help make me feel satiated." He asks Claudia to give him a bag off the vaporizer before explaining that he also sometimes drinks the "throwback" Pepsi sodas, which are made with sugar rather than corn syrup. He likes the taste of these and finds himself able to swallow them with no problems.

He even indulged in a rare beer recently. "On Sunday night, I asked Claudia to buy a six-pack of Miller Lite tallboys," he says, "and I took one sip and I was like *uhhh*, and then I thought about a sign advertising some high-end beer, and it said, 'Life's too short to drink cheap beer.' And I thought, you know what? That guy's *right*."

"I saw this before I was paralyzed," he adds, looking off mock-wistfully: "In that tender age between twenty-one and twenty-three."

I ask if he's had many visitors since moving here. Pearl Jam played here last November, the day after Thanksgiving. "When Eddie was in town for the concert, he spent like three afternoons with us, so that was awesome." Vedder spent a good part of Thanksgiving Day with Tomas, talking and watching movies. Tomas attended the concert the next day, but as usual had to leave early. Vedder, who lives in nearby Seattle, also provided assistance to help get Tomas and Claudia settled in Portland. An old friend from Kansas City has visited. Phil Donahue has come over twice—and Staff Sergeant Miltenberger, along with his wife, paid a visit recently. That *Nightline* piece they've been trying to shoot for the past year finally happened.

"It was good," says Tomas of Miltenberger's visit. "I got to talk to him a little bit. They spent a fair amount of time here, but you know, TV has to condense things to fit into the allotted time. He thought that I was going to shoot him when he walked through the door. I was like, 'Man, I could never shoot anybody, especially you.'"

A week ago was the tenth anniversary of Black Sunday. I ask Tomas if he did anything to commemorate the occasion. Tellingly, he can't remember. "I've tried to do something every April fourth," he says. "Did I do anything on April fourth this year?" He looks at the ceiling, asking himself and searching for an answer. "No, not particularly. I just figured it was the tenth year and I've run out of things to do."

Claudia brings over a can of formula and a syringe to feed Tomas. She lifts up his shirt, pops the gas from his colostomy bag, and begins to feed him as he talks. He tells me that his mother is currently down in Lubbock, Texas, visiting his newborn nephew, who is in the hospital after having problems breathing. He looks at his phone and reads aloud a text that said his nephew had improved and would be going home, probably today. He hands me the phone so I can see a photo of the baby.

Cathy has visited Portland, too. I ask Tomas how his relationship with his family is, now that he's moved away from Kansas City. "It's okay on the surface, up where everybody can see, it's all flowers and roses and butterflies, but underneath the surface, there is a bunch of bubbling distrust, and one party doesn't like another party, one doesn't trust the other one, it's . . ."

"Drama," I interject.

"Yeah," says Tomas. "I try to remain Switzerland. But it's good. Things are good." I tell him he sounds a lot better. "My oxygen's better, yeah," he responds. "I hate to break up the party, but can we take a break till tomorrow?"

The next morning at the hotel, I read with interest a front-page article in *USA Today* entitled "There Is Hope—Reversing Paralysis." It describes a stunning breakthrough in spinal cord injury research. Researchers testing a new procedure on a group of four patients who had complete SCI were able to restore voluntary movement to all of them. "By coursing electrical current through the four men's spines, the research team appears to have 'dialed up' signals between the brain and legs that were believed to be completely lost," the article reads. "All four men, after being paralyzed for two to four years, can lift their legs, flex their ankles and support their own weight while standing, though only when the device embedded under their skin is turned on. In a response that shocked researchers, all four have regained bladder and bowel control, sexual function and the ability to regulate their blood pressure and body temperature—even when the stimulation device is not running." I'm eager to share this incredible news with Tomas and to get his thoughts on it.

It's another warm, sunny day. I arrive around 9:30 a.m., after bumping into Claudia in the park near their apartment building during the walk over. Tomas is again in good spirits. "OK—ready to get to the soft, chewy nougat center of Tomas Young?" he quips as I turn on my voice recorder. "We've already made it through the hard, cheesy outer layer."

I mention the stunning news in *USA Today*. "Yeah," Tomas responds unexcitedly. "I got an email about that from this guy . . . about spinal implants." He's developed a level of skepticism when learning of new breakthroughs, even breakthroughs as staggering as those reported in today's news. "When I first got paralyzed," he says, "the people at Cal Berkeley said that they were doing work with stem cells and as soon as they're authorized to work on those who have scar tissue or a more difficult case then I'd be the first one on the list."

Tomas was excited at this news, but ultimately nothing happened. Hence the skepticism. Claudia points out that stem-cell research, a political issue, keeps stopping and restarting depending on which party is in power. Every time the research is reauthorized, researchers are back to square one—and with most trials, stem cell or otherwise, researchers tend to work with those who were recently injured, not older patients who have lived with their injuries for protracted periods, like Tomas. "What's disappointing is that if it comes, then they work on acute cases first, because of deterioration over time," she says.

Still, Tomas says he does try to keep up with new developments in spinal cord research, but he's reluctant to become emotionally invested, given the setbacks and complications he's endured over the past decade. "I'm like, well, if it becomes available, and they get these magic stem cells and implant them into my spine or whatever, and I could walk again, honestly, and this pains me to say it, but I don't know if I'm strong enough internally to deal with all the rehab, because I already had problems going through my first four years of being paralyzed, and then all of a sudden having the pulmonary embolism just when I was getting used to being a paraplegic and *pow*, I've got to get used to living in a new way and . . . I just . . . I don't know. I'd like to think that I'd be happy, but . . . I don't think I have the 'right stuff' inside me, so to speak, to persevere, to carry on. And who says that the stem-cell research holds for the rest of your life? They do that, and you start walking and do rehab, everything's fine, and *bam*, that part decides to shut down because it was rejected by your body or something."

Even setting aside the notion of regaining leg movement, Tomas says that the thought of recovering previously lost bodily functions isn't as meaningful to him anymore. One consideration is that the colostomy is not reversible. Another is his attitude toward sex, which he expressed to me during a conversation about the different types of catheters. Several years ago, he had considered undergoing a suprapubic catheter procedure, which surgically inserts a tube through the skin just above the pubic bone and into the bladder, as an alternative to the urethral catheter. Bobby Muller had advised him against it "because I wouldn't be able to get my dick up," Tomas explains, adding with pointed sarcasm, "which has become such a big part of my life, I can't tell you—you're lucky we weren't having sex when you walked in." Then, seriously, "We don't have sex anymore, we have a better relationship without sex, because . . . sex complicates things."

So given all he's endured, the notion of these dramatic developments is something Tomas is presently unwilling to entertain. He would rather devote his time to pursuits that are less emotionally risky, for now at least. Activism isn't one of them. He says he's taken a step back from working with IVAW. "I got out of the IVAW world when we got out of Iraq," he says. "If I had a choice, I'd make my own shirt that says, IVA*I*W—Iraq Veterans Against *Iraq* War. I thought the right war was in Afghanistan. And then when they caught bin Laden and killed him and buried his body at the bottom of the sea, I thought, well, now there's really no reason for us to stay in Afghanistan, but then I hear about the Taliban going to take over the country, and I'm like, well that's not really a good thing. So I don't know."

He's not yet involved with any peace or veterans' rights organizations in Portland. "Not at this time," he says, citing the fact that the van won't start and that the chaos of the move from Kansas City has not yet fully subsided. "Claudia said she kind of wants me to wait until we get completely settled before I call this guy in the VFP. 'Cause the state of Oregon just recently passed a law—public schools can have counter-recruiters. People who—they are like a recruiter at the school, but we have different information available." The concept of counter-recruiting is what Tomas spoke about during an IVAW board meeting several years ago. I ask him if he could imagine counter-recruiting being permitted back in Kansas City. "Fuck no," he responds.

I can see that Tomas is beginning to grow tired. I ask if he still tires frequently and takes naps during the day. "Oh yeah," he says. "Sometimes a lot. I'll start wanting to play a video game, and then during the video game, my eyelids become heavy and hard to keep open."

I ask if he ascribes the grogginess to one particular drug or some other cause. "It's just, my body is saying, man, you need, like, more time to make this feel right, so sleep as much as you can," he responds. "When you're awake, all the little workers aren't able to work because you're awake and all your systems are moving. I like to imagine my body as Fraggle Rock. And you know how they had all those little guys with the big noses and the hard hats that were always working on Fraggle Rock? I imagine that my body is filled with those guys, and they can only repair what's been broken when I'm asleep."

Tomas pulls on the vaporizer bag and asks, "So—any more probing questions?" His snark and sarcasm are on full display during this visit—more so than I've ever seen before. It's heartening to see him in such good spirits, even when I'm the victim of the barbs.

He tells me that he got a new wheelchair recently. It's sitting by the wall across from the foot of his bed. "They finally brought it yesterday," says Tomas, adding that it was due five months ago, "but when I sit back, those things," he points to the armrests, "they dig into my arms, so they have to get a new back." The chair also needs a chest strap to help keep his torso upright.

We talk a little more about the current situation in Afghanistan. "Hamid Karzai, who was in bed with the Taliban, doesn't want to sign the status of forces agreement that'll keep us there till 2024," he says, "because the Taliban wants to take over and start killing people—and it's around the time for elections, and all three of the people who are running against Karzai said they'd sign that agreement in a heartbeat to keep their people safer. So I don't know. There's a lot of political corruption in the Middle East, a lot of coercion."

Tomas begins rattling off one opinion after another on a variety of subjects, from war in the Middle East to marriage, demonstrating the sharp intellect and biting wit that made him such a powerful antiwar crusader. I picture him serving as a devastatingly effective counter-recruiter, if he can reach a point in his health where mobility isn't such a painful and daunting ordeal.

The next milestone for now, though, comes the next week, when Tomas and Claudia will celebrate their second wedding anniversary—an occasion that seemed unattainable this time last year.

Tomas is ready for a nap. We do the modified handshake, and I bid him farewell. He replies, "Goodbye, my friend." It's a scene that is frozen in my memory.

A few weeks later I talk to Nathan, who is encouraged that his older brother seems to be faring better since the move to Portland. He says the support Tomas received after the letter came out last year "gave him purpose again, and something to look toward, and I think moving to Portland was part of that," along with the availability of medical marijuana. "I think him living in downtown Portland is a big thing too," he adds, "because he lived in the suburbs of Kansas City and anywhere you had to go, you had to get in your van. And that was pretty painful for him, he didn't like getting in that van. Now that he lives in downtown Portland, he can go anywhere he wants, just roll down the street."

Nathan talks to his brother on the phone once every few weeks. His job as an oil rig instrumentation technician occupies much of his time, as do his two young children. "I work twelve days on, three to four days off, and I'm usually working probably twelve to fifteen hours a day," he says. "I work a lot, and it's just hard to keep in contact with him, and . . . I want to keep in touch with him more often, but . . ." But the two brothers' relationship remains close. "Yeah, I think it's in a good place, and we're in a place where we can go a couple of months without talking and start right back where we left off last time, so . . . we're pretty close like that."

Not too long after we spoke, Nathan received a package from Tomas in the mail. It contained a Purple Heart medal for his niece, Aleksus.

The two brothers soon saw each other again, this time in Boise at the funeral of their paternal grandfather, who died that July. This was the grandfather they had lived with for a year in California. "They were both very close to him; he was such a huge part of them growing up and becoming men, you know, because they really didn't have a good male role model," Cathy told me. "Their father was never a good role model, and they both went up there to the funeral and their father was there, which was unusual for them, because they haven't really seen him a lot." Indeed, it was the first time Tomas had seen his dad since he'd become paralyzed. They exchanged contact information and there were overtures between father and son to reconnect, but nothing came of it.

Cathy talks to her son on the phone every couple of weeks. "He doesn't call me; I have to call him," she says, "and his brother and sister, they call me. I don't go two, three days without Nathan calling me, and my daughter's over here once a week. But Tomas, I have to call him, and I kind of feel like—I kind of respect his . . . it's not really privacy, but, you know, respect where he is. What's going on with him. So we talk every couple, three weeks . . . and when we do talk, it's . . . an hour. You know, we've got a lot to catch up on, and that's good, you know; we laugh and we talk about the world and how shitty everything is, and his health."

I point out to her how much easier it is for me to understand his speaking voice on the phone compared to months past, and she agrees. "I think that he's in an ideal situation for him," she tells me. "You know, his house is set up purely for Tomas, and . . . he just seems to be at peace, and like you said, his speech—for so long, it was so hard to talk to him on the phone because you couldn't understand everything he said, and it was frustrating to him to keep saying 'What? What?' and you know, I hated to do that. I don't really know what to attribute that to other than the fact that he is taking different pain medication . . . you know, maybe part of it is just his emotional state is so much better now, too."

"I mean," she continues, "just looking back two years ago I couldn't have ever imagined that he would be where he is right now. And happy, and feeling good. But you know, when he was first paralyzed, and we didn't have any fucking clue what we were going to do, when we were sitting in the Target parking lot, leaving Saint Louis with a bag of pills in our hands and he had shit himself—no handicap van or handicap house. No clue what we were going to do. I said, 'The only way we're going to do this is together. But we will get through it.' And we did."

It's been a grueling journey for mother and son, but love is what got them through. "You know, when I was at Walter Reed, I don't know, maybe half a dozen days, and I was by myself in Washington,

D.C., and I would go over to the Fisher House and take a shower and come back over to the hospital, you know, I was spending seventeen, eighteen hours a day at the hospital, and one day—one of the unfortunate parts of PTSD is that you will lash out at the person closest to you, 'cause they're safe—one day, I don't even remember what it was, but he said something to me that was especially cruel, and I said, 'I'm going home. You do this by yourself. You want to be a dick, you can do this by yourself.' And I left and went back to the hotel, and did some laundry and came back, and he was all tears and hugs, and I'm like, 'You can't do this to me, I'm by myself in this, too.'" She adds, "So we've had some rough times, I'm not going to tell you that there's not been days that he hated me and I hated him, but I mean, I always felt like, you know, even with our movie, that was our love story. And bottom line, we just love each other; I would do anything for him, and he knows that. And so, yeah, as hard as it has been some days, we did it. . . . It all comes down to, he is my oldest and best friend."

Epilogue

The best people possess a feeling for beauty, the courage to take risks, the discipline to tell the truth, the capacity for sacrifice. Ironically, their virtues make them vulnerable; they are often wounded, sometimes destroyed.

—Ernest Hemingway

On November 19, 2014, I find myself driving west along a stretch of highway named the Purple Heart Trail, then north, past Worlds of Fun, where Tomas used to work, to northern Kansas City. Tomas's family and friends are gathering at a clubhouse in his mother's neighborhood, just a couple of miles away from his old house on Northeast 113th Street.

Nine days ago, on the eve of Veterans Day, Claudia woke up in the middle of the night in their new apartment in Seattle and immediately noticed that there was no sound from her husband. She checked on Tomas, as she had done many times before, but this time he was unresponsive. Peaches was at his side. Claudia remembers looking at the clock. It was 1:40 a.m. After a decade of hardship and pain, Tomas had died peacefully in his sleep.

The couple had moved to Seattle just a month earlier, due at least in part to some recent pain-management issues Tomas had been facing. The pain had worsened recently, and the Portland VA was unwilling to increase Tomas's medication. "We were running out of pills," said Claudia. Tomas was in near-constant pain again.

The last time I talked to Tomas was via telephone, just a few days before he moved to Seattle. In addition to hoping for a resolution to his pain issues, he said he was excited to be moving to an apartment close to the Experience Music Project and with a view of the Space Needle. He was looking forward to seeing Eddie Vedder more frequently; Vedder was set to visit him the day after Veterans Day and planned to provide more hands-on support now that Young was living in his hometown.

Tomas and I talked about this book and its progress; he was set to begin writing some essays for inclusion.

I talked to Claudia a few days after the news came. In addition to grieving the loss of her husband, she was trying to figure out how she was going to pay for his cremation; the VA would not pay until it was determined that the cause of Tomas's death was "service connected."

Claudia said that the novelty of moving to Seattle had quickly worn off when Tomas encountered the same resistance from the VA regarding pain management. Just as in the past—both in Portland and back in Kansas City—Tomas was forced to plead his case, to try to convince the medical staff how much pain he was experiencing. It often involved an ER visit, which Tomas abhorred. He had endured this all before and quickly became discouraged. Tomas had an appointment to meet with his doctor regarding the pain-management issues on November 24.

His death, however, was completely unexpected. While the precise cause was unknown, Claudia thinks he was simply exhausted from the pain and the battles with the VA. She is adamant that his death was not intentional, that Tomas would have contacted his family first if he planned to end his life intentionally—and, anyway, they were running out of pills. There weren't enough for a deliberate overdose.

◆

The gathering in Kansas City was a modest affair attended by friends and family. There was a table with framed photographs of Tomas, a couple of photo albums, and an arrangement of flowers. A copy of Eugene Richards's book, *War Is Personal*, lay open to the section on Tomas. A guestbook was available for guests to sign. Cathy brought a copy of the *Body of War* DVD and played it on a nearby TV. People gathered to talk about their lost friend, their lost son, their lost brother. Tomas's niece, Aleksus, played with a visiting veteran's PTSD service dog. Her mother held her baby brother, Michael Vincent Young, who shares the middle name of his uncle Tomas, whom he will never know.

Tomas Young was thirty-four years old.

Jacob George, the veteran of the war in Afghanistan who performed at the tribute show for Tomas in May 2013, committed suicide in September 2014.

Soldier's Heart

I'm just a farmer from Arkansas, there's a lot of things I don't understand
Like why we send farmers to kill farmers in Afghanistan
Now I did what I's told for my love of this land
I come home a shattered man with blood on my hands

Now I can't have a relationship, I can't hold down a job
Some may say I'm broken, I call it Soldier's Heart
Every time I go outside, I gotta look her in the eyes
Knowing that she broke my heart, and turned around and lied

Red, white and blue, I trusted you
And you never even told me why

It was 2002 and I just got off the Pakistan border to get out of the heat
My sergeant handed me orders and told me to read

It called for the mobilization of 500,000 soldiers, sailors and marines
For impending invasion of Iraq the coming spring
I got home a couple of months later and heard the drums of war
They had y'all dancing all around and asking for more

This soldier's heart couldn't take it anymore

Now I can't have a relationship, I can't hold down a job
Some may say I'm broken, I call it Soldier's Heart
Every time I go outside, I gotta look her in the eyes
Knowing that she broke my heart, and turned around and lied

Red, white and blue, I trusted you
And you never even told me why

Every time I go outside, I gotta look her in the eyes
Knowing that she broke my heart, and turned around and lied

Red, white and blue, I trusted you
And you never even told me why

You can listen to Jacob's music, read his writings, and donate to help share his message at www.jacobdavidgeorge.org.

References

The majority of the information in this book was gathered from interviews with those involved. I interviewed Tomas Young on several occasions at his home in Kansas City in 2013 and in Portland in 2014, in addition to frequently corresponding with him via telephone and email. The following individuals were also interviewed for the book: Claudia Cuellar, Phil Donahue, Roy McHugh, Tom Morello, Cathy Smith, Riley Soden, Ellen Spiro, Eddie Vedder, and Nathan Young.

Bauby, Jean-Dominique. *The Diving Bell and the Butterfly* (New York: Vintage, 1997).

Burns, John F. "7 US Soldiers Die in Iraq as a Shiite Militia Rises Up." *New York Times*, April 5, 2004, http://www.nytimes.com/2004/04/05/world/struggle -for-iraq-uprising-7-us-soldiers-die-iraq-shiite-militia-rises-up.html.

Cahill, Greg. "'Body' and Souls." *Pacific Sun*, April 11, 2008, https://www. highbeam.com/doc/1P3-1472240691.html.

Celizic, Mike. "Phil Donahue Unveils Documentary on Wounded GI." *Today*, NBC, April 1, 2008, http://www.today.com/id/23884161/ns/ today-today_news/t/phil-donahue-unveils-documentary-wounded-gi/#. VlzQsnarTrc.

Conniff, Tamara. "Q&A: Iraq Vet Tomas Young Finds Inspiration in Music." *Billboard*, March 7, 2008, http://mobile.reuters.com/article/ idUSN0735961520080309.

Doyle, Patrick. "Last Days of an Iraq War Hero." *Rolling Stone*, April 25, 2013.

———. "Tom Morello on Dying Veteran Tomas Young's Letter: 'There's

Nothing More Courageous.'" *Rolling Stone*, April 4, 2013.

Frankl, Viktor. *Man's Search for Meaning* (New York: Touchstone, 1984).

Gay, Patricia. "Tomas Young, Disabled Veteran, Tells Audience He'll Commit Suicide." *Ridgefield Press*, February 8, 2013.

Gillette, Felix. "Phil Donahue Strikes Back." *New York Observer*, June 20, 2007.

Goodman, Amy. "Body of War." *Democracy Now!*, March 27, 2008, http://www.democracynow.org/blog/2008/3/27/amy_goodmans_new_column_body_of_war.

Hedges, Chris. "The Crucifixion of Tomas Young." *Truthdig*, March 10, 2013, http://www.truthdig.com/report/item/the_crucifixion_of_tomas_young_20130310.

Hiatt, Brian. "Pearl Jam Kick Off Fall Tour." *Rolling Stone*, September 17, 2009.

Kelly, Alexander Reed. "Truthdigger of the Week: Jacob George." *Truthdig*, September 28, 2014, http://www.truthdig.com/report/item/truthdigger_of_the_week_jacob_george_20140928.

Kovic, Ron. *Born on the Fourth of July* (New York: Pocket, 1976).

Liu, Melinda. "Mean Streets." *Newsweek*, April 22, 2004.

Londoño, Ernesto. "Study: Iraq, Afghan War Costs to Top $4 Trillion." *Washington Post*, March 28, 2013, https://www.washingtonpost.com/world/national-security/study-iraq-afghan-war-costs-to-top-4-trillion/2013/03/28/b82a5dce-97ed-11e2-814b-063623d80a60_story.html.

Modell, Josh. "Pearl Jam Tour, Night 3: Chicago." *Spin*, August 25, 2009, http://www.spin.com/2009/08/pearl-jam-tour-night-3-brilliant-set/.

Morris, Frank. "Injured Veteran Keeps Up His Fight, Deciding to Live." KCUR, December 28, 2013, http://kcur.org/post/injured-veteran-keeps-his-fight-deciding-live#stream/0.

———. "Iraq War Veteran Tomas Young Signs Off with 'Last Letter.'" KCUR, March 28, 2013, http://kcur.org/post/iraq-war-veteran-tomas-young-signs-last-letter#stream/0.

NBC. *Meet the Press*. February 8, 2004, transcript, http://www.nbcnews.com/id/4179618/ns/meet_the_press/t/transcript-feb-th/.

Paul, Steve. "Paralyzed After a Firefight, Tomas Young Has Made Peace His New Mission." *Kansas City Star*, October 22, 2007.

Paynter, Ben. "A Tale of Two Soldiers." *Pitch*, March 2, 2006, http://www.pitch.com/kansascity/a-tale-of-two-soldiers/Content?oid=2181156.

PBS. *Bill Moyers Journal*. March 21, 2008, transcript, http://www.pbs.org

/moyers/journal/03212008/transcript1.html.

Raddatz, Martha. *The Long Road Home* (New York: Penguin, 2007).

Richards, Eugene. "War Is Personal: Tomas Young/Age 26/Kansas City, Missouri." *Nation*, March 27, 2006, http://www.thenation.com/article/war-personal-tomas-youngage-26kansas-city-missouri/.

Ricks, Thomas. *Fiasco* (New York: Penguin, 2007).

———. *The Gamble* (New York: Penguin, 2009).

Sendak, Maurice. *Where the Wild Things Are* (New York: HarperCollins, 1963).

Shanker, Thom. "'Stop-Loss' Will All but End by 2011, Gates Says." *New York Times*, March 18, 2009, http://www.nytimes.com/2009/03/19/washington/19gates.html?_r=0.

Slenske, Michael. "Body of Evidence." *Smith*, April 6, 2008, http://www.smithmag.net/obsessions/2008/04/06/back-home-from-iraq-with-tomas-young/.

Steinberg, James B., Michael E. O'Hanlon, and Susan E. Rice. "The New National Security Strategy and Preemption." Brookings Institution, policy brief, December 2002, http://www.brookings.edu/research/papers/2002/12/terrorism-ohanlon.

Stevenson, Richard W. "Antiwar Protests Fail to Sway Bush on Plans for Iraq." *New York Times*, February 19, 2003, http://www.nytimes.com/2003/02/19/international/middleeast/19IRAQ.html.

Szczepanski, Carolyn. "Anti-War Vet Tomas Young Hospitalized." *Pitch*, June 2, 2008, http://www.pitch.com/FastPitch/archives/2008/06/02/anti-war-vet-tomas-young-hospitalized.

———. "Body of War," *Pitch*, March 6, 2008.

Templeton, David. "A Body Meets a Body." *Pacific Sun*, January 17, 2012.

Trumbo, Dalton. *Johnny Got His Gun* (New York: Bantam, 1976).

Walshe, Shushannah. "Two Soldiers, Scarred by the Same Battle, Reunite 10 Years Later." ABC News, December 13, 2013, http://abcnews.go.com/US/soldiers-scarred-battle-reunite-10-years/story?id=21193704.

Weintraub, Karen. "There Is Hope: Reversing Paralysis." *USA Today*, April 8, 2014.

Wilder, Esther Isabelle. *Wheeling and Dealing: Living with Spinal Cord Injury* (Nashville, TN: Vanderbilt University Press, 2006).

Young, Tomas. "The Last Letter." *Truthdig*, March 18, 2013, http://www.truthdig.com/dig/item/the_last_letter_20130318.

Acknowledgments

When I first approached Tomas Young about writing this book back in early 2013, he said he'd be delighted for me to tell his story. He'd wanted to do it himself, but the embolism he suffered in 2008 robbed him of much of the use of his hands, and his ability to speak was too degraded for any voice-to-text software to be useful. Over the next few years, Tomas and Claudia opened their lives and their home to me and for this I am eternally grateful.

My sincere thanks to Cathy Smith for sharing her painful and personal memories with me, and for patiently answering my many follow-up questions as the book neared completion. Thanks also to Nathan Young for sharing his thoughts and memories with me.

My gratitude to Garett Reppenhagen for his patience and openness during my first couple of visits to Tomas's house, which coincided with his own. Thanks to Tomas's good friends Riley Soden and Roy McHugh for sharing their thoughts and stories, which helped bring the book to life.

Thanks to Tom Morello and Ellen Spiro for sharing their insight with me in interviews for the book.

Thanks to Eddie Vedder, who was recording "No More" back in 2007, around the same time that he wrote the foreword to my Pete Townshend book. That's how I learned of Tomas's story. My thanks also to Phil Donahue, another longtime passionate ally of Tomas.

Eddie and Phil have been important advocates for this project from beginning to end and I am deeply grateful.

I am immensely grateful to Shepard Fairey for donating such an incredible book cover, and to the photographers who graciously allowed the use of their beautiful and powerful images: Danny Clinch, Alan Messer, Olivier Morel, and Eugene Richards.

My sincere gratitude to Tomas and Claudia's good friend Nicole Vandenberg for supporting my book and sharing her valuable expertise and resources.

Thanks to my friends and family, who read early copies of the manuscript and provided valuable feedback.

Thanks to Geoff Millard, who put me in touch with Rory at Haymarket Books.

My deep gratitude to the team at Haymarket Books for their personal, enthusiastic (and patient!) support for this book – Rory Fanning, Julie Fain, Anthony Arnove, Jim Plank, Jason Farbman, Dao Tran, Rachel Cohen, Eric Kerl, and John McDonald. Thank you to editors Ruth Baldwin, Sarah Grey, and Brian Baughan for their expertise and insight.

Thanks to the family of Jacob George for allowing the use of his lyrics to "Soldier's Heart."

Thanks to my daughter Alex and sons Nick and Sam for their support, understanding, and love during the many hours that I ducked away to work on this book.

And my eternal thanks to my wife Melissa, who, as usual, was a sounding board through this entire project. I read every word of the book aloud to her as each chapter took shape, many times over. She laughed at Tomas's humorous stories and cried at the accounts of his often harrowing circumstances. She helped guide the book's structure and flow and lived this project right alongside me throughout, supporting me every step of the way.

Index

About Haymarket Books

Haymarket Books is a nonprofit, progressive book distributor and publisher, a project of the Center for Economic Research and Social Change. We believe that activists need to take ideas, history, and politics into the many struggles for social justice today. Learning the lessons of past victories, as well as defeats, can arm a new generation of fighters for a better world. As Karl Marx said, "The philosophers have merely interpreted the world; the point, however, is to change it."

We take inspiration and courage from our namesakes, the Haymarket Martyrs, who gave their lives fighting for a better world. Their 1886 struggle for the eight-hour day, which gave us May Day, the international workers' holiday, reminds workers around the world that ordinary people can organize and struggle for their own liberation. These struggles continue today across the globe—struggles against oppression, exploitation, hunger, and poverty.

It was August Spies, one of the Martyrs targeted for being an immigrant and an anarchist, who predicted the battles being fought to this day. "If you think that by hanging us you can stamp out the labor movement," Spies told the judge, "then hang us. Here you will tread upon a spark, but here, and there, and behind you, and in front of you, and everywhere, the flames will blaze up. It is a subterranean fire. You cannot put it out. The ground is on fire upon which you stand."

We could not succeed in our publishing efforts without the generous financial support of our readers. Many people contribute to our project through the Haymarket Sustainers program, where donors receive free books in return for their monetary support. If you would like to be a part of this program, please contact us at info@haymarketbooks.org.

Shop our full catalog online at www.haymarketbooks.org or call 773-583-7884.

About the Authors

Mark Wilkerson spent eight years in the US Army as an AH-1 Cobra and UH-60 Black Hawk helicopter crew chief with the 3rd Infantry and 101st Airborne Divisions. He was deployed with the 101st to Mogadishu, Somalia, for six months in 1993. Mark has three children: Alex, Nick, and Sam. He lives in Louisville, Kentucky, with his wife Melissa. He is the author of *Who Are You: The Life of Pete Townshend* and co-author of the *New York Times*-bestselling *Pearl Jam Twenty*. This is his third book.

Phil Donahue and the *Donahue* show have been honored with twenty Daytime Emmy Awards, including nine for Outstanding Host, and a George Foster Peabody Broadcasting Journalism Award. For his outstanding contribution to television and American culture, Mr. Donahue was inducted into the Academy of Television Arts and Sciences Hall of Fame on November 20, 1993.